DARK HORSES

ANNUAL 2014

MARTEN JULIAN

Raceform

Published in 2014 by Raceform Ltd.
High Street, Compton, Newbury, Berkshire, RG20 6NL

Copyright © Marten Julian 2014

The right of Marten Julian to be identified as the author of this work has been asserted by him in accordance with the Copyright, Designs and Patents Act 1988.

A catalogue record for this book is available from the British Library.

ISBN 978-1-909471-37-5

Designed by Fiona Pike and typeset by J. Schwartz & Co.

Printed and bound in the UK by CPI Group (UK) Ltd, Croydon, CR0 4YY

CONTENTS

INTRODUCTION 4

THE PREMIER LIST 5

THE DARK HORSES 29

THE DARK HANDICAPPERS 67

THE DERBY PREVIEW 81

THE OAKS PREVIEW 91

THE 1,000 GUINEAS PREVIEW 97

THE 2,000 GUINEAS PREVIEW 111

INDEX OF HORSES 127

INTRODUCTION

Thank you for buying the 2014 edition of the *Dark Horses Annual*. I hope that the book assists you through the season, and beyond, as both a useful source of reference and winners. If you are buying the publication for the first time here is a brief guide as to how the horses have been selected.

My Premier List horses are chosen in the expectation that they will reward support to level stakes by the end of the season. I also believe they have specific attributes that make them of special interest.

The Dark Horses are lightly raced and unexposed types, with more of a long-term future, while the Dark Handicappers are horses that I believe start the season on a favourable mark.

Please note that as the deadline for the book is early March, any news after that time relating to the featured horses or the Classics will not be accounted for. The reason I have written about certain horses that are not entered for the Classics is because they may be supplemented.

You can keep in touch with my latest thoughts about the horses featured in this book either through my services at www. martenjulian.com or by ringing my line (0906 150 1555), which is updated every day.

If you do not have internet access then ring Rebecca on 01539 741007 and register for our free postal newsletter. If you would like to discuss anything to do with this book then please email rebecca@ martenjulian.com and she will forward on your message to me.

I am, as always, indebted to Rebecca Dixon, Richard Lowther, James de Wesselow, Julian Brown, Jodie Standing, Steve Dixon, Natasha Julian, Hannah Julian and Paul Day for their help at various stages of the production.

Finally, I would like to wish you the very best of good fortune for the season and, once again, thank you for buying this publication.

Bye for now
Marten Julian

THE PREMIER LIST

The following horses, which have been drawn from a wide variety of backgrounds, are selected in the hope that they will reward support through the course of the season.

ASTONISHING (4YR BAY FILLY)

TRAINER:	**Sir Michael Stoute**
FORM:	**6/31221-**
PEDIGREE:	**Galileo – Amazing Krisken (Kris S)**
BHA RATING:	**109**
OPTIMUM TRIP:	**1m 4f**

Made rapid strides last season, progressing from a comfortable victory in a 1m 4f Class 5 maiden at Kempton in July to a seven-lengths' success in a Listed contest at Newmarket in September.

Shaped quite well on her sole start at two and again when third on her return in a 1m 2f Class 4 maiden at Newbury in June. Sneaked through a narrow gap to beat Respect Me with more in hand than the one and three-quarter length verdict would suggest when stepped up in trip next time for a 1m 4f Class 5 maiden at Kempton.

Caught close home on her handicap debut from a mark of 89 at Goodwood, looking sure to win until the last couple of strides. Again failed to hold the late thrust of the winner when beaten by Phaenomena in a 1m 4f Class 3 handicap at Newmarket in September from a mark of 92.

Raised in class into Listed company just five days later, and equipped for the first time with a ring bit, she showed significant improvement when coming from off the pace to pull seven lengths clear of Songbird in the 1m 4f Princess Royal Richard Hambro Stakes.

Raised 17lb, from a mark of 92 to 109, following that run and put away for the season.

Astonishing surging clear

By Galileo and a full sister to middle-distance Group 3 winner Sub Rose and other winners at shorter trips. Dam an unraced daughter of Kris S out of 1m Group 2 winner Magic Gleam.

Most progressive last autumn and has already shown more than enough ability to win at Group level. Likely to be aimed at the top middle-distance races for older fillies and may have more improvement still to come.

BALANSIYA (3YR BAY FILLY)

TRAINER:	**Dermot Weld**
FORM:	1-
PEDIGREE:	**Shamardal – Baliyana (Dalakhani)**
BHA RATING:	-
OPTIMUM TRIP:	**1m 2f +**

Hugely impressive winner of a 7f maiden in soft ground at Leopardstown in November, well away from the gate and settled in second before taking up the running on the home turn and drawing steadily clear, under hands and heels, to win by seven lengths.

Form hard to assess, but runner-up subsequently rated 80 so through her the winner ran to a mark in the mid-90s.

Balansiya – promises to be top class

By Shamardal and the first foal of Baliyana, winner of a 7f
maiden at two and then the Group 3 Derrinstown 1,000 Guineas
Trial at Leopardstown in May. Untried beyond a mile and ran last
on her only subsequent race in the Coronation Stakes.

Distaff side related to Bering, an influence for stamina, and bred
to be suited by quicker ground.

Showed plenty of pace at Leopardstown but entitled to improve
significantly over a mile or more. Already looks a top-class prospect
and has a fine action, so connections may be thinking of the Oaks
in June if she shows that she has the ability in the spring.

One of the most exciting prospects in the book.

BARLEY MOW (3YR BAY COLT)

TRAINER:	**Richard Hannon**
FORM:	**125-**
PEDIGREE:	**Zamindar – Harvest Queen (Spinning World)**
BHA RATING:	**110**
OPTIMUM TRIP:	**1m +**

Very highly regarded by connections but not seen at his best last season.

Justified strong market support when getting up close home under a confident ride from Richard Hughes to beat the useful Yuften by a neck in a 7f maiden at Newbury in August (third four and a half lengths away).

Caught out by the winner Be Ready's turn of foot next time in a 7f Listed race at Doncaster, staying on to finish three lengths back in second (not punished closing stages).

Again left out of his ground in the Group 1 Prix Jean-Luc Lagardere, held up in arrears and short of room when trying to make headway a quarter of a mile from home. Passed the post with plenty of running left in him.

Half-brother to 1m winner Glean out of a Listed 1m winning mare from the family of top-class performers North Light and Golan and top stayer Sought Out.

Bred to stay a mile and runs as if he will stay further. Still has plenty to prove on figures but leaves the strong impression he is a high class performer and could be one to keep in mind at long odds for a Group 1. Well suited by fast ground.

BIG THUNDER (4YR GREY GELDING)

TRAINER:	**Sir Mark Prescott**
FORM:	**0600/31211151-**
PEDIGREE:	**Dalakhani – Charlotte O Fraise (Beat Hollow)**
BHA RATING:	**98**
OPTIMUM TRIP:	**1m 4f +**

Would appear to be fully exposed, having run a dozen times over two seasons, but was still progressing towards the end of the autumn and may have scope to land one a top staying handicap.

Brought along steadily as a two-year-old, finishing down the field in four starts, and consequently started last season from a rating of 61. Beaten off that mark in a 1m 2f 0-65 at Leicester in May (possibly due to the soft ground) but made amends a few days later when making all to win a similar race next time at Brighton by eight lengths, eased down.

Found one too good for him under a 6lb penalty next time at Lingfield before responding to a hard ride to beat Salutation by a neck at Bath (75). Again required firm driving throughout when

Big Thunder – so tough and may still have more to offer

winning off 76 at Haydock before stepping up to a mile and a half a week later at Ascot, making all despite hanging off the bend and again in the straight (86).

Failed to confirm the form with Glenard next time from a mark of 94 before staying on gamely to beat Deficit by three-quarters of a length on his first attempt at one and three-quarter miles (93).

By Dalakhani out of a half-sister to a smart 1m winner in the Stakes, from the family of In The Wings, Dubawi and High-Rise.

Raised from 93 to 98 after winning at Haydock but relatively unexposed over 1m 6f and could be a likely type for a top staying handicap, perhaps the Ebor.

Improved 37lb last season and may have more to offer. Acts very well on fast ground.

BLUE HUSSAR (3YR BAY COLT)

TRAINER:	Aidan O'Brien
FORM:	1-
PEDIGREE:	Montjeu – Metaphor (Woodman)
BHA RATING:	-
OPTIMUM TRIP:	1m 2f +

May not be straightforward but only a good horse could have won as he did at Leopardstown in November.

Held up in arrears and niggled along from the outset, he had just two of his 13 rivals behind him on the turn for home. Finding his stride, he surged forward on the outside of the field to get up in the dying strides and win going away by three-quarters of a length.

The form of the race did not hold up and the time of the race was modest, but only a colt with a fair degree of talent could have won from such an unpromising position turning for home.

Distaff side mainly milers but shapes as if he will appreciate middle distances. Full brother won over a mile and a half out of a mare who was Listed placed over a mile.

Looked as if he would need at least a mile and a quarter this season. Displayed a visually impressive turn of foot in his maiden and could prove an interesting outside prospect for Group honours.

CARLA BIANCA (3YR GREY FILLY)

TRAINER:	**Dermot Weld**
FORM:	**24-**
PEDIGREE:	**Dansili – Majestic Silver (Linamix)**
BHA RATING:	**-**
OPTIMUM TRIP:	**1m 2f +**

Maiden after two starts but will almost certainly prove to be Group class, especially when asked to tackle middle distances.

Had the misfortune to come up against Australia on her debut at the Curragh in July, a little flattered to get within three-quarters of a length of the winner having pulled five lengths clear of the third. Stepped up considerably in class into Group 1 company in September for the Moyglare Stud Stakes, staying on to finish just over four lengths fourth under considerate handling.

First foal of an unraced half-sister to Profound Beauty, a winner of nine races at Listed and Group 3 level up to 1m 6f, from the family of Ribblesdale Stakes winner Irresistible Jewel.

Excelled to run so well against more precocious fillies in the Moyglare in view of her inexperience.

May not have the pace to compete against the best at a mile, but bred to relish middle distances and may well prove good enough to be competitive in top company at a mile and a half.

CLOUDSCAPE (3YR BAY COLT)

TRAINER:	John Gosden
FORM:	1-
PEDIGREE:	Dansili – Set The Scene (Sadler's Wells)
BHA RATING:	-
OPTIMUM TRIP:	1m 2f +

Hugely impressive winner of his sole start at two, coming from well behind to win a 1m Class 5 maiden by three lengths pulling away.

Third foal and a half-brother to 1m 2f winner Playbill out of a 1m 4f winning half-sister to useful middle-distance performer Rosslyn Castle, 1m 4f winner Magog and Marywell from the family of Irish Oaks winner Margarula.

Form hard to assess, but seventh won next time and both he and the eighth are now rated on 70. That would put this colt on a mark in the mid to high 80s.

Looks very useful and likely to be effective at Pattern-class level. Sure to stay a mile and a half and perhaps further.

CURIOUS MIND (4YR BAY FILLY)

TRAINER:	Sir Mark Prescott
FORM:	1-
PEDIGREE:	Dansili – Intrigued (Darshaan)
BHA RATING:	-
OPTIMUM TRIP:	1m 2f +

Once-raced four-year-old filly with the potential to make significant progress when stepped up in trip.

Very green from flagfall and outpaced for much of the race when making a belated racecourse debut in a 1m Class 5 maiden at Southwell in December. Looked held for much of the race until stamina started to kick in, eventually asserting and staying on well to win by a length and a half.

Did well to win over a mile given her stout pedigree. By Dansili and a half-sister to 1m 3f Listed winner and St Leger third Michelangelo and 1m 4f winner No Heretic, so looks sure to relish a step up to middle distances.

Second now rated on 67, so ran to a figure in the low 70s and would look very interesting from that mark in a 1m 2f or more handicap.

Has size and scope and could not be in better hands. Looks sure to reward the patience of her connections.

ERTIJAAL (3YR BAY COLT)

TRAINER:	**William Haggas**
FORM:	**21-**
PEDIGREE:	**Oasis Dream – Shabiba (Seeking The Gold)**
BHA RATING:	**98**
OPTIMUM TRIP:	**7f +**

Had the misfortune to come up against subsequent Group 1 winner Toormore on his debut at Leicester in May, beaten a neck and finishing seven lengths clear of the third (now rated on 79) after a troubled run.

Looked very useful when beating Exceeder, now rated 80, on the bridle by six lengths in a 6f Class 5 contest at Yarmouth in June.

By Oasis Dream out of a 1m Listed winning daughter of Seeking The Gold, suggesting he will be best suited to trips up to a mile.

Has a strong fast-ground bias to his pedigree and not short of speed. Definitely Group class and promises to hold his own at the highest level. Travels well and has a turn of foot.

INDY (3YR BAY COLT)

TRAINER:	**David Barron**
FORM:	**1-**
PEDIGREE:	**Indian Haven – Maddie's Pearl (Clodovil)**
BHA RATING:	**95**
OPTIMUM TRIP:	**7f +**

Responded bravely to firm driving to beat 8/15 chance Penny Drops in a 6f maiden stakes on his racecourse debut at Doncaster in November.

Looked held by smooth-travelling favourite entering the final furlong, but responded bravely to some stern reminders and won going away by four lengths. Runner-up had finished second in a Listed race at Newmarket eight days earlier and third later beaten in poor company at Wolverhampton, so form is hard to assess.

Half brother to a sprint winner in Spain out of a half-sister to Group-placed Excelerate and a French Listed winner over a mile and a quarter.

Needed every yard of this six furlongs and looks very likely to stay a mile. Handled the soft ground well.

David Barron – an underrated handler

Not many options open to him from a mark of 95, but evidently a colt of some potential and likely to figure at some point in Listed or even Group class.

INTEGRAL (4YR BAY FILLY)

TRAINER:	**Sir Michael Stoute**
FORM:	**11012-**
PEDIGREE:	**Dalakhani – Echelon (Danehill)**
BHA RATING:	**115**
OPTIMUM TRIP:	**1m +**

A filly of the highest class, who looks sure to win a Group 1 race at some point this season.

Unraced at two, she made an immediate impression on her debut in a 1m maiden at Goodwood in May, quickening on the far side to win by two and three-quarter lengths.

Integral (right) battling up the hill at Sandown

Rated on 88 and stepped up to Listed company next time, met rivals rated up to 19lb superior and beat them emphatically with a show of speed from well off the pace to win going away by a length and a half.

Raised 16lb, to 104, and stepped up again in grade for the 1m 2f Group 1 Nassau Stakes but in a very rough race failed to get a clear run and finished seventh. Made amends next time when dead-heating with the gutsy Ladys First in a 1m Group 3 at Sandown.

Confirmed that she is a Group 1 filly when running the best race of her career in the 1m Sun Chariot Stakes at Newmarket, leading a furlong out but caught close home by Sky Lantern, again running above her rating (raised from 109 to 115).

By Dalakhani and a half-sister to Elysian, a winner over a mile and a half. Dam, Echelon, a Group 1 winner over a mile and reached her peak as a five-year-old. From the family of Group 2 winner Chic and 2,000 Guineas winner Entrepreneur.

Officially improved by 27lb last season and may have more to offer, especially if given another try over a mile and a quarter. Has a turn of foot, a great attitude and a very likeable way of galloping.

Acts well on fast ground and confidently expected to prove herself at the highest level.

LADY HEIDI (3YR BAY FILLY)

TRAINER:	**Philip Kirby**
FORM:	**431-**
PEDIGREE:	**High Chaparral – Water Feature (Dansili)**
BHA RATING:	**97**
OPTIMUM TRIP:	**1m 2f +**

Showed progressive form in three runs last season, culminating in a battling defeat of Safety Check in a 1m Listed contest run in heavy ground at Pontefract in October.

Shaped adequately on her debut at Thirsk in September, staying on steadily to finish fourth to Comino in a 7f maiden. Improved on that 13 days later over a mile at Newcastle, plugging on steadily to finish third to the potentially top-class Volume.

Lady Heidi – relishing the mud at Pontefract

Took a significant step up in class just over a month later, starting 20/1 against colts rated in the high 90s. Held up off the pace, made steady headway two furlongs out and stayed on strongly in the final furlong to win going away by two and three-quarter lengths.

Extremely well bought at 22,000gns as a two-year-old given her decent pedigree and subsequent form. By High Chaparral and the fourth foal of an unraced daughter of Dansili related to an Italian Oaks runner-up from the family of Tenby and Shining Water.

Handled cut in the ground well last season and bred to thrive over middle distances. Already useful, rated 97, and may well be seen at her best in the spring and autumn when she is more likely to have underfoot conditions to suit her.

Every chance that she will enhance her trainer's growing reputation.

LADY TYNE (3YR CHESTNUT FILLY)

TRAINER:	Roger Charlton
FORM:	51-
PEDIGREE:	Halling – Susan Kelapa (St Jovite)
BHA RATING:	90
OPTIMUM TRIP:	1m 2f +

Allayed concerns about her acting on the heavy ground when landing a 1m Class 4 at Newbury by eight lengths from a filly now rated 73.

Had shaped nicely on her debut at Kempton in August, staying on steadily to finish fifth.

The 10th foal of a 1m 1f winning daughter of St Jovite and a half-sister to five winners including Military Power, St Oswald, Monsusu, Non Ultra and Royal Composer – all best at distances up to a mile and a quarter.

Handled the testing ground well at Newbury in view of the strong fast-ground bias on both sides of her pedigree.

Left the impression she has the potential to earn black type at some point this season, probably over a mile and a quarter or more. Should be even better on quicker ground.

LIGHTNING SPEAR (3YR CHESTNUT COLT)

TRAINER:	Ralph Beckett
FORM:	1-
PEDIGREE:	Pivotal – Atlantic Destiny (Royal Academy)
BHA RATING:	-
OPTIMUM TRIP:	7f +

Made a very good impression when displaying an impressive turn of foot to win a 7f maiden at Kempton on his racecourse debut in August.

Travelled smoothly just off the pace before being produced under hands and heels by Jamie Spencer to challenge and then quicken through to win by three-quarters of a length, appearing to pass the post with plenty in hand.

Mixed messages from the form – the fourth Fracking won later in the season and is now rated on 82 – but the colt had been doing nice work at home and the win came as no surprise.

By Pivotal, costing 260,000gns as a yearling, and is a half-brother to several winners at trips up to a mile and a quarter including Ocean War, Seaway and Atlantic Light. Dam, a winner over five and six furlongs, is a half-sister to 1m 2f Group 2 winner Make No Mistake.

Family not short of speed but from the evidence of Kempton a mile should not be a problem.

Lines through the third and fourth suggest he ran to a mark in the high 80s, which may encourage connections to start him in a handicap.

Had Group 1 entries at two and entered for the Irish 2,000 Guineas this year. A tall horse, with a likeable way of racing at Kempton and evidently expected to progress to better things. May prove best at up to a mile for the time being.

MUWAARY (3YR BAY COLT)

TRAINER:	John Gosden
FORM:	1-
PEDIGREE:	Oasis Dream – Wissal (Woodman)
BHA RATING:	82
OPTIMUM TRIP:	1m +

Had subsequent winners behind him when winning a 7f Class 4 maiden at Newbury in July, beating Torrid (now rated 89) by half a length with something in hand.

Looked a little green, travelling just off the pace, but came through smoothly and showed a bright turn of foot to assert, doing just enough to win.

Sixth foal and closely related to Ethaara, winner of three of her five starts including a 6f Listed contest, and 7f Listed winner Mudaaraah out of an unraced half-sister to Bahri.

May have been underrated on 82 given the subsequent form of the race. Not bred to stay further than a mile and has a strong fast-ground bias to his pedigree.

May be aimed at a handicap in the light of his possibly favourable BHA rating, but has the potential to move above that grade.

MY TITANIA (3YR BAY FILLY)

TRAINER:	John Oxx
FORM:	211-
PEDIGREE:	Sea The Stars – Fairy Of The Night (Danehill)
BHA RATING:	106
OPTIMUM TRIP:	1m +

Progressive filly, who displayed fine battling qualities when holding the late run of Chicago Girl in the Group 3 CL Weld Park Stakes at the Curragh in September.

Just over three weeks earlier she had won in a similar style at Leopardstown, leading a quarter of a mile from home and staying on strongly to hold the persistent challenge of Afternoon Sunlight by two and a quarter lengths.

My Titania – could be anything

Form did not work out particularly well but both races were run in good times.

By Sea The Stars out of a mare who won at nine furlongs and is herself a half-sister to 1m 4f Grade 3 winner Dress Rehearsal.

Tends to do only enough to win but bred to be suited by a mile or more and there was talk of the Oaks after her second success.

Has a very likeable attitude and appeals as the sort to keep improving through the season. Looks versatile regarding ground and has the potential to go a long way.

OBLITERATOR (3YR BROWN COLT)

TRAINER:	**Ger Lyons**
FORM:	**1-**
PEDIGREE:	**Oratorio – Faraday Light (Rainbow Quest)**
BHA RATING:	**-**
OPTIMUM TRIP:	**1m 2f +**

Could be the horse to put his trainer's name on the map in the UK.

Made a successful debut in a 1m maiden at the Curragh in September, mid-division for much of the race before responding to quiet urgings to run on steadily and win going away by two and a half lengths.

Only managed to find his stride inside the final furlong, as you would expect given his pedigree. Half brother to Irish 1,000 Guineas winner Just The Judge and another winner over a mile out of a half sister to Group 3 winner and Oaks third High Heeled.

Form nothing special, with runner-up now rated on 82, third beaten a long way just under a fortnight later at Dundalk and fourth also beaten next time out.

Looks as if he has more in the way of stamina than Just The Judge and may require at least a mile and a quarter to show his best.

May not be easy to place but certainly warrants an early crack at a trial. Should come to himself over middle distances in the summer. A very interesting prospect.

POSTPONED (3YR BAY COLT)

TRAINER:	Luca Cumani
FORM:	512-
PEDIGREE:	Dubawi – Ever Rigg (Dubai Destination)
BHA RATING:	96
OPTIMUM TRIP:	1m +

Did well to show such useful form over seven furlongs at two given that everything about him is crying out for trips of a mile or more.

Shaped nicely on his debut in a 7f maiden at Newmarket in July, running green before staying on steadily in the final furlong. Well backed and overcame signs of inexperience to beat a subsequent 84-rated rival in second (Miner's Lamp, winner of his next two starts, fourth now on 95) in a 7f Class 5 maiden at Yarmouth.

Stepped up in class for the £500,000 Tattersalls Millions 2yr Old Trophy over seven furlongs next time at Newmarket he again impressed, responding to firm driving to snatch second in a line of four at the post.

By Dubawi and the second foal of a half-brother to a horse placed over 1m 3f. The dam, a winner over 1m 4f, is a half-sister to the dam of a US winner over 1m 2f and the 1m 5f winner Bite Of The Cherry.

Has a powerful way of galloping and handles quick ground. Already rated 96 and looks sure to figure at Group-class level, probably over a mile and a quarter and beyond.

RENEW (4YR BAY COLT)

TRAINER:	Marco Botti
FORM:	64/121231-0
PEDIGREE:	Danisili – Hold Me Love Me (Sadler's Wells)
BHA RATING:	105
OPTIMUM TRIP:	1m 4f +

Imposing son of Dansili, who impressed last season as a horse with the scope to improve beyond handicap class.

Bought out of Aidan O'Brien's yard for 48,000gns at Tattersalls in October 2012 after showing a little ability in the second of his two runs as a juvenile.

Made a successful debut for these connections when staying on strongly up the straight at Thirsk to beat Street Artist, Chancery (rated 81) and Tetbury (rated 82). Ran well on his handicap debut from a mark of 85 next time at Newmarket, staying on in the final furlong despite being short of room.

Kept on very well next time in July, hooded for the first time, leading three furlongs out and again staying on strongly to win a 1m 4f 0-85 at Doncaster by three-quarters of a length. Raised 8lb, from 85 to 93, and beaten on the nod by Glenard in a 1m 4f Class 2 handicap at Haydock. Raised a further 5lb, from 93 to 98, and stepped up in trip to 1m 6f, finished a fair third to Nearly Caught (not suited by the soft ground).

Showed that he was ready for a rise in grade when tackling a 1m 4f Listed race at Newmarket in September, taking a while to pick up until pulling clear inside the final furlong to beat Wigmore Hall by a length.

Dam, by Sadler's Wells, won at 1m 5f and is a full sister to Irish 1,000 Guineas winner Yesterday, Moyglare Stud Stakes winner Quarter Moon and 1m 2f winner All My Loving – all three placed in the Oaks.

Now rated on 105 and looks sure to make his presence felt at Group level. More a galloper than a horse with gears but very game and really likes fast ground.

Could go a long way this summer.

RYE HOUSE (5YR BAY GELDING)

TRAINER:	**Sir Michael Stoute**
FORM:	**00/412/1-**
PEDIGREE:	**Dansili –Threefold (Gulch)**
BHA RATING:	**98**
OPTIMUM TRIP:	**1m 2f +**

Has not been straightforward, running just six times in three seasons, but has always had ability and could thrive as a five-year-old especially if tackling his favoured soft ground.

Shaped with a little promise when in arrears in two runs at two (2011) and again showed something on his seasonal debut at three, earning an opening handicap mark of 75. Stepped up to a mile and a half, battled on gamely to beat Man Of Plenty by a head.

Looked sure to defy a 7lb rise next time at Salisbury, quickening three lengths clear before tying up close home and beaten a head by Rule Book.

Made a winning return last season, dropped back to 1m 2f for a Class 3 handicap at York, drawing clear and winning by three and a quarter lengths off 88.

Not seen out again and has to start the new season from a mark of 98.

A half-brother to 1m 4f winner Jedi, Park Hill Stakes winner Hi Calypso and 1m 4f winner Warringah. Capable of winning over a mile and a quarter but bred to appreciate further.

May be good enough to earn black type when racing with ease in the ground. More a galloper than a horse with gears, but lightly raced with the scope to progress again.

Andrew Balding – has a good team this year

SCOTLAND (3YR BAY COLT)

TRAINER:	**Andrew Balding**
FORM:	31-
PEDIGREE:	**Monsun – Sqillo (Bachelor Duke)**
BHA RATING:	**96**
OPTIMUM TRIP:	**1m 2f**

Very interesting son of Monsun, who confirmed the promise shown on his debut in a 1m maiden at Sandown in September when powering away with a Class 3 contest over the extended mile at Epsom just over a fortnight later.

Made a pleasing impression there, travelling smoothly on the outside of the field before edging left down the camber as he came through to beat rivals rated 95, 94, 93 and 99 with plenty in hand.

Looks reasonably treated on 96, taking strict lines of form, but is probably destined for Pattern-class races.

First foal of a half-sister to nine winners, most of them over a mile. Has always shown pace at home, but his sire is an influence for stamina so he should stay a mile and a quarter and will probably get the mile and a half. Appreciated the cut in the ground on both starts and has the physical scope to improve.

Has a bright future and the potential to earn black type, especially later in the season when he matures and has his ground. Very progressive sort and one to stay with.

TAGHROODA (3YR BAY FILLY)

TRAINER:	John Gosden
FORM:	1-
PEDIGREE:	Sea The Stars – Ezima (Sadler's Wells)
BHA RATING:	89
OPTIMUM TRIP:	1m 2f +

May have caught connections on the hop when staying on nicely under hands and heels riding to beat the 89-rated Casual Smile by a neck in a 1m Class 4 maiden at Newmarket in September, with subsequent winner Tea In Transvaal (rated 79) in third.

By Sea The Stars and the second foal of triple Listed winner, up to 1m 6f, who is a half-sister to Listed placed Ezalli from the family of 1m 4f Listed winner Ebaziya, dam of Group 1 winners Enzeli, Edabiya and Estimate.

Comes from a well-established family of classy stayers and looks sure to appreciate middle distances. Likely to prove way superior to her mark of 89 and has to be considered as a possible Oaks candidate.

Did things very nicely at Newmarket and has the potential to become a top-class staying filly. Very exciting.

TRUE STORY (3YR BAY/BROWN COLT)

TRAINER:	**Saeed Bin Suroor**
FORM:	**21-**
PEDIGREE:	**Manduro – Tanzania (Darshaan)**
BHA RATING:	**100**
OPTIMUM TRIP:	**1m 4f**

Looked a staying type, as you would expect from his pedigree, when powering up the hill to win the best maiden of the season at Newmarket on his second outing in July.

Had shaped with promise over the same course and distance the time before, running on into second behind subsequent Dewhurst Stakes third and Breeders' Cup Juvenile Turf winner Outstrip, now rated 117. Winner had the better turn of foot close home.

Form of True Story's maiden could hardly have worked out better. Second home Expert subsequently won twice (now rated 99), third Voice Of A Leader won next time and then Listed placed, fourth Rock 'N' Roll Star has since won, fifth Postponed won next time and is included in this section (now rated 96), sixth, eighth and 10th also subsequent winners.

Did really well to win over seven furlongs given his stout pedigree. Half-brother Serengeti won over a mile and a quarter and dam, a daughter of Darshaan, is from the family of Oh So Sharp.

True Story – could be top class over middle distances

Looked short of a gear last season but has an admirable attitude and the pedigree to excel over middle distances.

Has the credentials to warrant a Derby preparation. One of the most promising horses in this section.

VOLUME (3YR BAY FILLY)

TRAINER:	**Luca Cumani**
FORM:	**311-**
PEDIGREE:	**Mount Nelson - Victoire Finale**
	(Peintre Celebre)
BHA RATING:	**86**
OPTIMUM TRIP:	**1m 4f**

Extremely promising daughter of Mount Nelson, with the potential to progress to Group-class races.

Shaped like the best horse in the race when staying on third to Enraptured (now rated 86) in 7f Class 4 maiden at Newmarket in August.

Started 8/11 for a 1m Class 5 maiden at Newcastle just under a month later and won comfortably by four and a half lengths despite racing a little keenly in the early stages. Form worked out well, with second now rated on 73 and third on 97.

Improved again on her third start, staying on strongly to beat Gold Trail by one and a quarter lengths in a 1m 1f 0-90 nursery from a mark of 80.

Half-sister to full brothers Validus, best over a mile despite being bred for middle distances, and Velox out of a 1m winning half-sister to 1m 7f Group 2 and St Leger second Vertical Speed from the family of a 2m 4f Prix du Cadran winner.

Gallops with a rounded action and stays rather than quickens, but bred to thrive over middle distances and likely to prove superior to her mark of 86. Trainer is very effective with a horse of this type.

THE DARK HORSES

The following horses, mostly lightly raced or unraced, have shaped with sufficient encouragement either on the track or at home to merit inclusion in this section.

ABSEIL (4YR BAY COLT)

TRAINER:	Sir Michael Stoute
FORM:	Unraced
PEDIGREE:	First Defence –Intercontinental (Danehill)
BHA RATING:	-
OPTIMUM TRIP:	7f +

Unraced four-year-old but, perhaps significantly, kept in training as an entire.

By Grade 1 Forego Stakes winner First Defence, sire of Grade 1 winning filly Close Hatches and Group 3 winner Dundonnell, out of top-class French and US performer Intercontinental.

Dam has not yet produced anything to match her talent since retiring to stud, but this colt would not have been kept in training had he not shown sufficient ability to warrant the patience.

AGE OF INNOCENCE (3YR BAY COLT)

TRAINER:	Andre Fabre
FORM:	1-
PEDIGREE:	Invincible Spirit – Elusive Legend (Elusive Quality)
BHA RATING:	-
OPTIMUM TRIP:	7f +

One of a handful of French horses included in the book this year.

Landed the odds when beating subsequent winner Zlatan Dream in a 6f newcomers' race at Maisons-Laffitte in July. Form nothing special, but well regarded by his trainer and should prove competitive at trips up to a mile at a decent level.

Second foal of US winner at two from the family of Kentucky Derby winner Street Sense and top sire Mr Greeley.

Plenty of pace in his pedigree and worth noting if he turns up in the UK at some point.

ALYASAN (3YR CHESTNUT COLT)

TRAINER:	**John Oxx**
FORM:	**Unraced**
PEDIGREE:	**Sea The Stars – Alaya (Ela-Mana-Mou)**
BHA RATING:	-
OPTIMUM TRIP:	**1m 4f**

Half-brother to many useful performers including Alayan, Alaivan, Alzari and Alayuir out of a 1m 4f winning half-sister to Alamshar from the family of Aliysa.

Has been given plenty of time to grow into himself but has always shown his trainer that he has some ability. One to note for the midsummer targets over middle distances.

ARAB SPRING (4YR BAY COLT)

TRAINER:	**Sir Michael Stoute**
FORM:	**2-**
PEDIGREE:	**Monsun – Spring Symphony (Darshaan)**
BHA RATING:	-
OPTIMUM TRIP:	**1m 4f +**

Evidently not been straightforward, having raced just once in two years, but shaped well on his racecourse debut racing keenly in arrears. Had no problem when the pace quickened three furlongs from home, momentarily baulked for a few strides before switching wide and coming with a steady run to finish second, beaten two and a half lengths by Elkaayed.

Sir Michael Stoute – looks set for a good season

The winner was rated 83 following that race and after good efforts in two Group 3 races on his final two starts ended the season on a mark of 106.

By Monsun out of a 1m 4f winning daughter of Darshaan and a sister to Hard Top and Conduit. Half-brother to useful performers Glass Harmonium, Fruehling and Holda.

Ran to a mark in the low 80s on the strength of this effort but will prove better than that, especially when given the chance to tackle middle distances.

Comes from a very successful slow-maturing middle-distance family. Could not be in better hands to thrive as a four-year-old and likely to improve as the season progresses provided his problems are behind him.

ASTRONEREUS (3YR CHESTNUT COLT)

TRAINER:	**Amanda Perrett**
FORM:	**Unraced**
PEDIGREE:	**Sea The Stars – Marie Rheinberg (Surako)**
BHA RATING:	-
OPTIMUM TRIP:	**1m 4f +**

Fifth foal and a half-brother to four winners including 2009 Prix du Jockey Club winner Le Havre, 1m 2f winner Scarlet And Gold and 1m winner Alamarie. His dam is an unraced half-sister to the top-class Polar Falcon.

Bred along staying lines and likely to come into his own towards the second half of the season.

ASYAD (3YR BAY FILLY)

TRAINER:	**Sir Michael Stoute**
FORM:	**41-**
PEDIGREE:	**New Approach – Elle Danzig (Roi Danzig)**
BHA RATING:	-
OPTIMUM TRIP:	**1m 2f**

Imposing filly with plenty of scope, who shaped well on her debut at Salisbury in September before making all to win a 1m Class 5 maiden in soft ground at Yarmouth.

By New Approach and the ninth foal of Elle Danzig, winner of 11 Group races from a mile to a mile and a half. Closely related to a 1m 2f Listed winner and a half-sister to other useful performers at around the same distance.

Has plenty of size and looks sure to stay a mile and a quarter, perhaps further. Well regarded last season and likely to be tackling Group class races at some point.

AYRAD (3YR CHESTNUT COLT)

TRAINER:	Roger Varian
FORM:	Unraced
PEDIGREE:	Dalakhani – Sweet Firebird (Sadler's Wells)
BHA RATING:	-
OPTIMUM TRIP:	1m 2f +

Fifth foal and a half-brother to three winners including But Beautiful, both best at around six furlongs. The dam, a winner over a mile and a quarter and Group 3 placed, is a sister to 1m 2f Listed winner Moscow Ballet and closely related to the top sprinter Stravinsky. The second dam is Fire The Groom, a winner of five races here and then the Beverly D Stakes in America.

A nice-moving colt that has impressed his handler. Bred for middle distances but does not lack pace.

BASEM (3YR BAY COLT)

TRAINER:	Saeed Bin Suroor
FORM:	Unraced
PEDIGREE:	Pivotal – Gonbarda (Lando)
BHA RATING:	-
OPTIMUM TRIP:	1m +

Brother to the hugely talented Farrh and 1m 2f winner Welcome Gift. Dam was a Group 1 winner over a mile and a half in Germany and is a sister to 1m to 1m 2f performer Gorlor.

Shapes nicely and expected to win races at a reasonable level.

BOY IN THE BAR (3YR CHESTNUT GELDING)

TRAINER:	David Barron
FORM:	6-
PEDIGREE:	Dutch Art – Lipsia (Dubai Destination)
BHA RATING:	-
OPTIMUM TRIP:	1m ?

Eye-catching in a 6f maiden at Haydock in September on his sole
start, well behind and nudged along before finishing with a late
flourish when the race was over.

Second foal of a half-sister to a 1m 2f Listed winner from the
family of Prince of Wales winner Two Timing.

Appeared to show a turn of foot on his debut, quickening to pass
four rivals inside the final furlong. One of the most interesting
horses in this section and likely to be placed to advantage by his
astute handler.

DANJEU (3YR BAY COLT)

TRAINER:	John Gosden
FORM:	0-
PEDIGREE:	Montjeu – Wanna (Danehill Dancer)
BHA RATING:	-
OPTIMUM TRIP:	1m 2f +

Incredibly green through the race when eventually staying on to
finish seventh of 12 in a 1m maiden at Newmarket in October.
Slowly away and last early on, wandered around and had to be
switched several times at halfway before finding his stride a
furlong out and doing his best work close home, never nearer than
at the line.

Expensive at 725,000gns, he is the first foal of his dam Wanna, a
winner over a mile and a half and a full sister to 1m Listed winner
Pirateer from the family of Cheveley Park winner and 1,000
Guineas second Wannabe Grand.

Stayed the mile well here and will appreciate further. Bred to appreciate a little cut in the ground.

Likely to be brought along steadily through the ranks, but has the potential to move beyond handicap class.

DARK DAYS (3YR BAY COLT)

TRAINER:	Paul Cole
FORM:	Unraced
PEDIGREE:	Black Sam Bellamy – Darwinia (Acatenango)
BHA RATING:	-
OPTIMUM TRIP:	1m 2f +

Seventh foal and a full brother to German 1m 3f Listed and US Grade 2 winner Daveron, and a half brother to 7f winner Don Libre. Dam, a winner at 1m 3f, is a sister to the dam of Animal Kingdom.

Has shown ability at home and expected to win races at a decent level.

EBANORAN (3YR BAY COLT)

TRAINER:	John Oxx
FORM:	1-
PEDIGREE:	Oasis Dream – Ebadiyla (Sadler's Wells)
BHA RATING:	-
OPTIMUM TRIP:	1m +

Won with more in hand than the head margin suggests when always holding the late challenge of Table Rock in a 7f maiden at the Curragh in October.

By Oasis Dream and the 10th foal of Irish Oaks and French Leger winner Ebadiyla, a half-sister to Enzel and Ascot Gold Cup winner Estimate.

The dam has produced a number of winners including Eyshal and 1m 4f and hurdle winner Ebaziyan.

Stayed the seven furlongs well at the Curragh and promises to get further.

Enjoyed a tall reputation last season and will probably start in a Guineas trial before a decision is made about targets. Likeable.

EBASANI (3YR CHESTNUT COLT)

TRAINER:	**John Oxx**
FORM:	**1-**
PEDIGREE:	**Manduro – Ebatana (Rainbow Quest)**
BHA RATING:	**-**
OPTIMUM TRIP:	**1m 4f**

Looked very professional when landing a 1m maiden on yielding ground at Navan in October, challenging approaching the final furlong and keeping on well at the finish to hold the late run of 4/9 favourite Belisarius.

Did well to win given his stamina-based pedigree. By Manduro out of Ebatana, a daughter of Rainbow Quest out of a winner of the Irish Oaks and French Leger. Dam has produced dual-purpose performer Ebadiyan and the useful Listed-placed Ensaya,

Sure to relish a test of stamina and may prove good enough to race at Group-class level when asked to tackle a mile and a half or more.

Ebasani – on her way to victory at Navan

ECONOMY (4YR GREY GELDING)

TRAINER:	**Sir Michael Stoute**
FORM:	**2-**
PEDIGREE:	**Dalakhani – Quiff (Sadler's Wells)**
BHA RATING:	-
OPTIMUM TRIP:	**1m 4f +**

Imposing son of Dalakhani, unraced at two, who shaped very well on his sole start last season but did not appear again.

Appeared in a 1m 4f maiden at Lingfield in July, travelling well in the early stages and making steady progress turning for home despite running green. Had just struck the front when swamped by the late run of Buchanan, coming away with the winner and beaten a head after pulling five lengths clear of the third.

Mixed messages in relation to the form, with the winner subsequently twice beaten in handicaps off 82 and the 79-rated Lions Park seven lengths behind in fourth.

Half-brother to a winner over six furlongs but dam won the Yorkshire Oaks and finished second in the St Leger. Has plenty of scope to improve and bred to stay well. May not have been easy to train, but would not have been kept in training without good reason. Sure to win a maiden at least and clearly has much more to offer.

EMIRATI SPIRIT (3YR BAY COLT)

TRAINER:	**Roger Varian**
FORM:	**Unraced**
PEDIGREE:	**New Approach – Dance Lively (Kingmambo)**
BHA RATING:	-
OPTIMUM TRIP:	**1m +**

Sixth foal and a half-brother to a handful of winners including 1m 5f Listed winner Charleston Lady, Japanese 1m Group 3 winner Live Concert, 1m winner Tap Dance Way and a winner in Greece.

Bred along miling lines but expected to stay further.

END OF LINE (3YR BAY COLT)

TRAINER:	**Andrew Balding**
FORM:	1-
PEDIGREE:	**Pastoral Pursuits – Just Devine (Montjeu)**
BHA RATING:	**89**
OPTIMUM TRIP:	**1m +**

Appears to have caught connections a little by surprise when coming with a smooth run from off the pace to win a 7f maiden on soft ground at Doncaster in October.

Form hard to evaluate, but could not have won any easier and evidently relished the ease in the ground.

By Pastoral Pursuits and the third foal of a half-sister to a Group 3 1m 4f winner by Montjeu. This colt a half-brother to triple-6f winner Magic Secret.

Bred for pace from his sire but stayed the trip well at Doncaster and may well get a mile and a quarter, perhaps middle distances.

End Of Line – has a future

Ensuring (far side) – winning at Sandown from Early Morning

ENSURING (3YR BROWN COLT)

TRAINER:	**James Fanshawe**
FORM:	**10-**
PEDIGREE:	**New Approach – Dynacam (Dynaformer)**
BHA RATING:	**87**
OPTIMUM TRIP:	**1m 2f +**

Did his best work in the closing stages on both his starts, coming with a strong late run to beat Early Morning by a neck on his racecourse debut at Sandown in August.

Ran to a mark of around 80 there (those behind subsequently rated in the mid 70s), but won with more in hand than the narrow verdict would suggest.

Took a step up in class next time out, tackling the £500,000 Tattersalls Millions 2yr Old Trophy at Newmarket. Slowly away and outpaced three furlongs out, he then found his stride and ran on very strongly to finish seventh, five lengths behind the winner and never nearer than at the line.

Half-brother to a 6f winner who was placed over a mile and a
half, out of a mare who won over 1m 2f at two and is a half-sister to
Breeders' Cup Juvenile winner Action This Day and 1m 6f winner
Sicily.

Seems fairly treated on 87 given the marks of those around him
at Newmarket. Bred for trips beyond a mile and runs as if he needs
further, so every chance that he will improve when asked to tackle a
mile and a quarter or more.

Has a pleasing way of racing and may be the right type for a
valuable mid-summer handicap.

ENZANI (3YR BAY COLT)

TRAINER:	John Oxx
FORM:	Unraced
PEDIGREE:	Cape Cross – Eytarna (Dubai Destination)
BHA RATING:	-
OPTIMUM TRIP:	1m 2f +

First foal of a middle-distance winning half-sister to Ascot Gold
Cup winners Enzeli and Estimate, Irish Oaks and French Leger
winner Ebadiyla and Moyglare Stud Stakes winner Edabiya.

Comes from one of the Aga Khan's best bloodlines and expected
to enhance the family name.

EVITA PERON (3YR CHESTNUT FILLY)

TRAINER:	Ralph Beckett
FORM:	Unraced
PEDIGREE:	Pivotal – Entente Cordiale (Ela-Mana-Mou)
BHA RATING:	-
OPTIMUM TRIP:	1m +

Unraced daughter of Pivotal and the seventh foal of a daughter
of Ela-Mana-Mou who stayed a mile and a half (related to a 3m
hurdle/chase winner).

Half-sister to several winners including King's Stand winner Equiano, 1m winner Elvira Delight, six-race winner Orife and 1m 3f winner Barahir.

Mixed messages from her pedigree but pleased her trainer last season and should stay at least a mile.

FOREVER NOW (3YR BAY COLT)

TRAINER:	**John Gosden**
FORM:	**0-**
PEDIGREE:	**Galileo – All's Forgotten (Darshaan)**
BHA RATING:	-
OPTIMUM TRIP:	**1m 4f**

Full brother to 1m 5f Group 3 winner Shantaram and 2,000 Guineas third Gan Amhras out of a mare that won over a mile.

Steadily got the message on his debut in a 1m maiden at Kempton, behind before plugging on at one pace up the far rail to finish never nearer in eighth.

Looked an out-and-out stayer here, with the scope to make significant improvement as a three-year-old.

GALLANTE (3YR BAY COLT)

TRAINER:	**Andre Fabre**
FORM:	**1-**
PEDIGREE:	**Montjeu – Crazy Volume (Machiavellian)**
BHA RATING:	-
OPTIMUM TRIP:	**1m +**

Won a 1m maiden for unraced colts and geldings at Longchamp in September on his sole start. Form subsequently shown to be ordinary, but is highly regarded and will probably appear in the UK at some stage given he is owned by Messrs Smith, Magnier and Tabor.

Third foal and a full brother to 1m 5f Flat and hurdle winner Plinthy. Dam won in the States over six furlongs and is a half-sister to 1m 4f winner Fortuni, 1m 2f winner Unique Pose and 1m 3f winner Endless Expanse.

Will probably stay beyond a mile and could be useful.

GAMESOME (3YR BAY COLT)

TRAINER:	**Olly Stevens**
FORM:	**01-**
PEDIGREE:	**Rock Of Gibraltar – Hot Coal (Red Ransom)**
BHA RATING:	**98**
OPTIMUM TRIP:	**6f +**

Hardly thrown in on an opening mark of 98, but clearly has loads of ability and promises to become a very useful performer at trips up to a mile.

Showed a hint of his ability in a 7f maiden on his racecourse debut in August but evidently came on a bundle for that run when quickening to beat Speedfiend by three lengths, despite drifting left, in a 6f maiden just 13 days later at Nottingham.

Runner-up was not disgraced in Group 1 Middle Park Stakes on his final start (rated 105), so the form looks way superior to the regular run-of-the-mill Nottingham maiden.

By Rock Of Gibraltar and a half-brother to winners up to 1m 2f, out of a dam related to milers.

Did well to win on the soft going as there is a strong bias to fast ground on both sides of his pedigree. May stay a mile but showed plenty of pace at Nottingham and could prove best at around six furlongs.

Has the potential to earn black type at some point.

Gm HOPKINS (3YR BAY COLT)

TRAINER:	**John Gosden**
FORM:	**40-**
PEDIGREE:	**Dubawi – Varsity (Lomitas)**
BHA RATING:	-
OPTIMUM TRIP:	**1m 2f**

Twice-raced son of Dubawi, who is bred to thrive over trips of a mile and a quarter and more.

Eye-catching on his debut in a 6f maiden at Newbury in May, travelling smoothly in arrears and then making steady headway on the rails to finish full of running in fourth, beaten a fast-diminishing length.

Never travelling in a similar race over the same trip at Newmarket in June, finishing 12th of 15 beaten 28 lengths by Jallota, who had been upsides this colt at Newbury.

Defeat may have been due to the quick ground and an issue with a foot, which has since been addressed.

First foal of a 1m 4f winning half-sister by Lomitas to a 1m 2f Listed winner in Italy from the family of Mark Of Esteem.

Bred to stay middle distances, so did exceptionally well to show such promise over six furlongs on his debut.

Requires a third run for a handicap mark and will prove of great interest when stepped up to a mile or more. In the right hands to win a decent handicap or two.

HADAATHA (3YR GREY FILLY)

TRAINER:	Roger Varian
FORM:	Unraced
PEDIGREE:	Sea The Stars – Hathrah (Linamix)
BHA RATING:	-
OPTIMUM TRIP:	1m 2f +

Unraced but highly regarded last season.

By Sea The Stars out of 1,000 Guineas third Hathrah, a half-sister to five winners including UAE 2,000 Guineas winner Stagelight and useful middle-distance Ivan Luis. Dam, a winner of the 1m Masaka Stakes, is a daughter of Linamix, a strong influence for stamina.

This filly, a half-sister to 2m winner Itlaaq, has a rock-solid middle-distance pedigree.

HORS DE COMBAT (3YR CHESTNUT COLT)

TRAINER:	James Fanshawe
FORM:	12-
PEDIGREE:	Mount Nelson – Maid For Winning (Gone West)
BHA RATING:	91
OPTIMUM TRIP:	6f +

Displayed a very willing attitude when beating Rosehill Artist and Inchila in a 7f auction maiden stakes on his racecourse debut at Newmarket in August. Travelled well just behind the leaders, switched to challenge and then quickened to lead and ran on to win by one and three-quarter lengths.

Started 1/4 to follow up in a 7f Class 4 conditions race at Kempton and beaten a neck by Evening Attire despite battling bravely all the way to the line. Winner rated highly by connections and time will show there was no disgrace in that defeat.

Second foal of a half-sister to US 1m 1f Grade 1 winner Stroll and the useful US winner Patrol. Despite winning over seven furlongs that trip may prove a little beyond his best.

Has plenty of speed on the distaff side of his pedigree and may prove effective back at six furlongs.

IDEA (3YR GREY COLT)

TRAINER:	Sir Michael Stoute
FORM:	U1-
PEDIGREE:	Mizzen Mast – Discuss (Danzig)
BHA RATING:	78
OPTIMUM TRIP:	7f

Unseated his rider at the start on his debut at Goodwood in September then made amends in a 6f Class 5 maiden at Windsor, doing well to win comfortably in the end after having to be switched for a run approaching the final furlong.

Half-brother to 1m and Listed-placed Argumentative out of a Listed-placed daughter of Danzig from the family of Sanglamore.

Mixed messages from his pedigree, but overall feeling is that a mile will be the limit of his stamina. Won with more in hand than the half-length margin would suggest and likely to prove superior to his opening mark.

Handled soft ground well at Windsor but has a pedigree predisposed to quicker ground. Interesting to see where he starts.

JORDAN PRINCESS (3YR BAY FILLY)

TRAINER:	Luca Cumani
FORM:	01-
PEDIGREE:	Cape Cross – Princess Nada (Barathea)
BHA RATING:	79
OPTIMUM TRIP:	1m 2f +

Shaped with promise, making late headway from arrears, on her debut at Kempton in September and confirmed that potential just under a month later in a 1m Class 5 maiden at Newcastle, making headway two furlongs out to win comfortably by two and three-quarter lengths from a filly now rated on 73.

Half-sister to a 1m 2f winner out of a Listed winning half-sister to Dubawi from the family of Italian Oaks winner Zomaradah and Derby winner High-Rise.

Bred to stay beyond a mile and every chance she will get a mile and a half. Opening mark reasonable based on her form, but surprising if she does not progress beyond it through the season.

KATILAN (3YR BAY COLT)

TRAINER:	John Oxx
FORM:	Unraced
PEDIGREE:	Cape Cross – Katiyra (Peintre Celebre)
BHA RATING:	-
OPTIMUM TRIP:	1m 2f +

Sustained a setback early last season but rated highly by his handler and could take high rank over middle distances.

First foal of a 1m 2f Group 2 winner daughter of Peintre Celebre from the family of 7f winner Katrisa, 1m 5f winner Kayalar and 1m 4f winner Katiola from the family of Derby winner Shahrastani.

Likely to be brought along quietly by his patient handler with a view to peaking in the second half of the season.

KISANJI (3YR BAY COLT)

TRAINER:	Mick Channon
FORM:	0-
PEDIGREE:	Teofilo – Al Kamah (Kingmambo)
BHA RATING:	-
OPTIMUM TRIP:	1m +

Well regarded by his trainer and kept on quite well on his debut in a 1m maiden at Salisbury, racing in mid-division and then staying on without quickening in the heavy ground.

Third foal out of an unraced daughter of US Grade 1 winner Catinca.

Not really bred to stay much further than a mile and may be best kept to that trip initially. One of the nicer prospects in his yard.

LACAN (3YR BAY COLT)

TRAINER:	Clive Cox
FORM:	Unraced
PEDIGREE:	New Approach – Invincible Isle (Invincible Spirit)
BHA RATING:	-
OPTIMUM TRIP:	1m

Unraced son of New Approach and the first foal of a 7f winning daughter of Invincible Spirit from the family of 1m 4f winner Oxford Line.

Took time to come to hand last season, but pleased his trainer in the work he did and is one to note when he appears on the track. Unlikely to stay much beyond a mile.

LAT HAWILL (3YR BAY COLT)

TRAINER:	Marco Botti
FORM:	1-
PEDIGREE:	Invincible Spirit – Arbella (Primo Dominie)
BHA RATING:	-
OPTIMUM TRIP:	7f ?

Not easy to assess given the ease of his success in a 7f Class 4 maiden at Newcastle on his sole start last season.

Held up just off the pace, he made smooth headway to take the lead a quarter of a mile out and pull clear to win by eight lengths from subsequent winner Poetic Choice (now rated on 72). Ran to a mark in the high 80s there but not seen out again.

Must have impressed in the Breeze-Up sale, selling for 230,000gns having cost just 10,000gns as a yearling.

Third foal of a 1m 4f Listed winning half-sister to very useful dual-purpose performer Overturn from the family of Group 1 winner Connaught Bridge. Half-brother to 1m 6f winner Chocola. Stayed the seven furlongs well last season and should get a mile, perhaps further.

Bred for quick ground and has an interesting future.

MADAME CHIANG (3YR BAY FILLLY)

TRAINER:	David Simcock
FORM:	1-
PEDIGREE:	Archipenko – Robe Chinoise (Robellino)
BHA RATING:	-
OPTIMUM TRIP:	1m 2f

Really did catch the eye with a most taking debut in a 1m maiden at Yarmouth in October, outpaced and looking very green for much of the way until coming with a late flourish in the final furlong to win going away by four lengths.

A half-sister to a 1m 4f and 2m 3f hurdle winner out of a middle-distance winning half-sister to a Listed winner over a mile and three-quarters.

No collateral lines to the form yet, so hard to assess the merit of the performance, but appealed as a filly with the potential to progress to better things over a distance of ground. Acted well in the soft going.

MANGE ALL (3YR BAY GELDING)

TRAINER:	**William Haggas**
FORM:	**3-**
PEDIGREE:	**Zamindar – Blancmange (Montjeu)**
BHA RATING:	-
OPTIMUM TRIP:	**1m 2f +**

Could hardly have run a more encouraging race on his debut in a 1m maiden at Newmarket in October, nudged along from arrears at halfway and staying on steadily up the rising ground to finish a fast-closing third, beaten a nose and a short head.

First foal of an unraced half-sister to an Italian 1m 2f winner and a winner over seven furlongs, out of a Listed winner over six furlongs related to a stayer.

Not devoid of speed on his distaff side, but stayed the mile in the soft ground very well at Newmarket and looks sure to get further in time.

A lovely maiden to start the season and may progress beyond handicap company in time.

MIN ALEMARAT (3YR CHESTNUT COLT)

TRAINER:	Marco Botti
FORM:	Unraced
PEDIGREE:	Galileo – Baraka (Danehill)
BHA RATING:	-
OPTIMUM TRIP:	1m 2f +

Fourth foal and a full brother to Beyond Conceit, a winner over an extended 1m 2f at two and later a mile and a half. Dam won the Lingfield Oaks Trial and is a full sister to top Japanese filly Fine Motion and a half-sister to Pilsudki.

Shaped well in early work last season and could prove one of the yard's better colts.

MAHSOOB (3YR BAY COLT)

TRAINER:	John Gosden
FORM:	Unraced
PEDIGREE:	Dansili –Mooakada (Montjeu)
BHA RATING:	-
OPTIMUM TRIP:	1m 2f +

Unraced son of Dansili and the first foal of a 1m Listed-placed daughter of Montjeu who stayed a mile and a half. Dam a half-sister to a 1m winner from the family of Group 3 winner and 1,000 Guineas third Bint Shadayid, from the family of 1,000 Guineas winner Shadayid.

Shaped well on the gallops last season and bred to appreciate a mile and a half. May have the potential to earn black type at some point.

MUNAASER (3YR BAY COLT)

TRAINER:	Sir Michael Stoute
FORM:	3-
PEDIGREE:	New Approach – Safwa (Green Desert)
BHA RATING:	-
OPTIMUM TRIP:	1m + ?

Sure to come on leaps and bounds from his introduction at Yarmouth last September, where he did good late work to finish third to Oxsana, subsequently second in Listed company and not disgraced this winter in Meydan.

Form further upheld by runner-up Torchlighter, a winner of a 6f maiden by seven lengths eight days later at Pontefract.

Son of New Approach and the second foal of a 1m winning full sister to Almuktahem and a half-sister to middle-distance performer Maraahel and Group-placed Huja.

Dam by Green Desert, so may struggle to stay beyond a mile despite an entry for the Derby.

Left the impression last season that he was a colt of some potential.

NAADIRR (3YR BAY COLT)

TRAINER:	Marco Botti
FORM:	01-
PEDIGREE:	Oasis Dream – Beach Bunny (High Chaparral)
BHA RATING:	82
OPTIMUM TRIP:	1m +

Showed only a modicum of promise on his debut in a 7f maiden at Newmarket in October, running green in arrears and struggling in the soft ground.

Looked a different horse just under a month later in a 7f Class maiden at Kempton, making all and quickening away on the bridle to win by two and a half lengths with something in hand.

By Oasis Dream and the first foal of a 1m 2f winning half-sister to a sprint winner from the family of Prix Marcel Boussac winner Miss Tahiti, who stayed a mile and a half.

Sire's stock strongly predisposed to quick ground so could be one to keep in mind for top races through the summer.

Form stood up well, with third, fourth, fifth, sixth and last subsequently winning races. Consequently could be favourably treated on 82 and may be capable of earning black type.

Bred to stay a mile but does not lack pace. Has plenty more to offer.

NIGHT FEVER (3YR BAY FILLY)

TRAINER:	John Gosden
FORM:	Unraced
PEDIGREE:	Galileo – Ask For The Moon (Dr Fong)
BHA RATING:	-
OPTIMUM TRIP:	1m 2f

Unraced full sister by Galileo to Derby third Astrology out of a daughter of Dr Fong that won the Group 1 Prix Saint-Alary.

Showed promise at home last season and expected to make an impression over middle distances, perhaps at a reasonably decent level.

NORAB (3YR BAY COLT)

TRAINER:	Marco Botti
FORM:	4-
PEDIGREE:	Galileo – Night Woman (Monsun)
BHA RATING:	-
OPTIMUM TRIP:	1m 4f

Looked to be going nowhere for much of the straight on his debut in a 1m maiden at Nottingham last November before finishing with a flourish when the race was all but over to snatch fourth.

Marco Botti – his team gets stronger every year

Closely related to three winners in German including Group 1 1m 4f winner Night Magic and others. Dam is a granddaughter of German Oaks winner Novelle.

Looked an out-and-out stayer at Nottingham, in accordance with his pedigree. May be the type to bring along steadily.

OBSERVATIONAL (3YR CHESTNUT COLT)

TRAINER:	Roger Charlton
FORM:	2-
PEDIGREE:	Galileo – Party (Cadeaux Genereux)
BHA RATING:	-
OPTIMUM TRIP:	1m 2f +

Shaped well when a close second to Chatez, now rated 78, in a 1m Class 4 maiden at Newbury in late October. Kept on well to the line and pulled two lengths clear of the third.

Closely related to Party Line, a winner at up to 1m 6f, out of a mare who won a 7f Listed contest from the family of a French Group 3 winner.

Has more than enough ability to win a maiden, possibly with the potential to progress to better things. Displayed a likeable attitude at Newbury.

PELERIN (3YR CHESTNUT FILLY)

TRAINER:	**Marco Botti**
FORM:	1-
PEDIGREE:	**Shamardal – Fragrancy (Singpsiel)**
BHA RATING:	-
OPTIMUM TRIP:	**1m 2f +**

One of a handful of horses to impress on the all-weather surface, showing a smart turn of foot in a 7f maiden at Kempton in October to quicken three lengths clear of what may prove to be a moderate field.

Second foal of a 1m and 1m 2f winner from the family of a 2,000 Guineas fourth and the family of top-class filly Hibaayeb.

Tenuous links suggest she ran to a mark in the low 80s but she looks better than that. Likely to improve when asked to tackle a mile or more. Could be very useful.

RAPPROCHEMENT (3YR BAY COLT)

TRAINER:	**Charlie Appleby**
FORM:	**Unraced**
PEDIGREE:	**New Approach – Firth Of Lorne (Danehill)**
BHA RATING:	-
OPTIMUM TRIP:	**1m 2f +**

A half-brother to four winners including UAE Oaks winner Falls Of Lora and French 1m Listed winner Etive. Dam useful in France and the States from the family of Cherry Hinton winner and 1,000 Guineas runner-up Kerrera.

Has shown promise in his work to date and could prove one of Godolphin's better colts.

ROYAL BATTALION (3YR BAY COLT)

TRAINER:	Olly Stevens
FORM:	Unraced
PEDIGREE:	Sea The Stars – Yummy Mummy (Montjeu)
BHA RATING:	-
OPTIMUM TRIP:	1m 2f +

Cost 575,000gns as a yearling and a half-brother to middle-distance winner Another Cocktail. Dam, a winner at 1m 2f, is a full sister to Irish Derby and Ascot Gold Cup winner Fame And Glory.

Extremely well bred and shows enough to raise hopes that he will not disgrace the family name.

SARPECH (3YR BAY COLT)

TRAINER:	Sir Mark Prescott
FORM:	0-
PEDIGREE:	Sea The Stars – Sadima (Sadler's Wells)
BHA RATING:	-
OPTIMUM TRIP:	1m 2f +

Slowly away before being bustled along to race in mid-division in a 1m Class 5 maiden at Nottingham in October, losing his place early in the straight and not punished thereafter.

Not cheap at 430,000gns as a yearling and a half-brother to six winners including top-class performer Youmzain, Group 1 winner Creachadoir and Group 3 winner Shreyas. Dam, a winner over a mile and a quarter, is from the family of Pilsudski.

Bred to stay well and is sure to leave his debut effort far behind.

SEAGULL STAR (3YR BAY GELDING)

TRAINER:	William Haggas
FORM:	1-
PEDIGREE:	Sea The Stars – Dash To The Top (Montjeu)
BHA RATING:	81
OPTIMUM TRIP:	1m 2f +

Very interesting son of Sea The Stars, who caught connections by surprise when comfortably landing a 1m Class 4 maiden at Newmarket on his debut last October.

Always travelled well and moved into the lead approaching the final furlong, beating a rival now rated on 78 by one and a quarter lengths with something in hand.

Cost 190,000gns and bred to appreciate middle distances, out of a daughter of Montjeu who won a 1m 2f Listed race.

Trainer says the colt needs fast ground, so likely to thrive in the summer months. Hard to assess but has the pedigree and potential to merit a Derby entry.

SEA PRIDE (3YR BAY FILLY)

TRAINER:	Sir Mark Prescott
FORM:	Unraced
PEDIGREE:	Sea The Stars – Claxon (Caerleon)
BHA RATING:	-
OPTIMUM TRIP:	1m 2f +

Unraced daughter of Sea The Stars out of Claxon, a Group 2 winner over a mile and a quarter and a Listed winner three times.

Dam has produced four winners at stud, notably Group 3 winner and Group 1 Nassau Stakes runner-up Cassydora, Listed winner Classic Remark and dual-winner and Listed placed Clarietta.

Bred to stay middle distances and one to note towards the second half of the season.

SHANKLY (3YR BROWN COLT)

TRAINER:	Clive Cox
FORM:	10-
PEDIGREE:	Monsun – Miracle Seeker (Rainbow Quest)
BHA RATING:	81
OPTIMUM TRIP:	1m 2f +

Looked an unlikely winner at halfway on his debut in a 1m novice stakes at Salisbury in September, slowly away and pushed along before delivering a strong run to beat Faintly (rated 82) going away by three-quarters of a length.

Raised significantly in class two months later for the 1m 2f Group 1 Criterium de Saint-Cloud, but beaten 32 lengths in testing ground.

Bred to stay, by Monsun and the first foal of middle-distance Listed winner Miracle Seeker, a half-sister by Rainbow Quest to Champion Hurdle winner Katchit and 3m hurdle/chaser winner Prince Erik.

Shankly – in very capable hands

Has a stamina-packed pedigree, so did very well to win over a mile. Defeat in France probably best attributed to the soft ground (trainer not one to overface his horses).

Holds Classic entries this season and could be an exciting sort for midsummer races over a mile and a quarter or more. Sure to be placed to optimum effect by his talented handler.

SINKAL (3YR BROWN COLT)

TRAINER:	**Dermot Weld**
FORM:	**Unraced**
PEDIGREE:	**Smart Strike – Sindirana (Kalanisi)**
BHA RATING:	-
OPTIMUM TRIP:	**1m 2f**

Unraced son of Smart Strike and the third foal of Listed middle-distance winner Sindirana, a half-sister to useful staying types from the family of Derby winner Sinndar.

Sire, a winner of eight races in the US, has proved a great success at stud with Curlin and US Grade 1 winners English Channel, Fabulous Strike and many more.

Has the pedigree of a miler or ten furlong horse. Showed his trainer something at home last season and bred to be suited to fast ground.

STAMPEDE (3YR BAY COLT)

TRAINER:	**Sir Michael Stoute**
FORM:	**0-**
PEDIGREE:	**High Chaparral – Summerhill Parkes (Zafonic)**
BHA RATING:	-
OPTIMUM TRIP:	**1m +**

Showed a little more than his finishing position suggests when last of 13 in a 7f Class 5 maiden at Sandown in August, shuffled along from halfway and staying on steadily under hands and heels riding.

Cost 100,000gns as a yearling and is a half-brother to a handful of winners at distances ranging from seven furlongs to two miles. Dam, a Listed winner over six furlongs, is a half-sister to multiple sprint winner Lucky Parkes.

Has a slightly imbalanced look to his pedigree and may be best at seven furlongs for the time being. Has apparently had a good winter and should run well in an early maiden before progressing to better things.

SWEEPING UP (3YR BAY FILLY)

TRAINER:	**Hughie Morrison**
FORM:	**23-**
PEDIGREE:	**Sea The Stars – Farfala (Linamix)**
BHA RATING:	**-**
OPTIMUM TRIP:	**1m 2f +**

Twice-raced maiden, who shaped a little better than her finishing position suggests in two starts at Leicester and Nottingham.

Stayed on well in a 1m maiden when second to Surcingle at Leicester in September and then third, not given a hard time, to Cambridge in a 1m maiden at Nottingham.

By Sea The Stars and a half-sister to six winners including Park Hill runner-up Starfala and 1m 2f Listed winner Under The Rainbow out of a 1m 4f Listed winning sister to Group 1 winners Fragrant Mix and Alpine Rose.

Has a long way to go to live up to her breeding, but certain to improve for a step up to a mile and a half and will be brought along quietly by her trainer.

May earn black type before the end of the season.

John Quinn – has an interesting prospect in Tahira

TAHIRA (4YR CHESTNUT FILLY)

TRAINER:	John Quinn
FORM:	31430-
PEDIGREE:	Doyen – Tennessee Queen (Big Shuffle)
BHA RATING:	-
OPTIMUM TRIP:	1m +

Daughter of Doyen and a very interesting recruit to this yard, having shown useful form in Germany.

Won a maiden at Hanover in May, a valuable 1m contest at Hamburg in July and a 1m 2f event back at Hanover in September. Also ran fifth in a 1m 1f Listed race at Baden-Baden.

Bred along miling lines but evidently gets a mile and a quarter and handles cut in the ground. Be interesting to see at what level she is pitched.

UNFORGIVING MINUTE (3YR BAY COLT)

TRAINER:	Clive Cox
FORM:	Unraced
PEDIGREE:	Cape Cross – Ada River (Dansili)
BHA RATING:	-
OPTIMUM TRIP:	1m +

Unraced 120,000gns son of Cape Cross and the first foal of Listed-placed 1m winner Ada River, a sister to useful performers Balducci and Listed winner Dont Dili Dali.

Mare by Dansili, so may stay beyond a mile.

Showed his trainer a fair level of ability last season and can win a maiden before progressing to better things.

VALLADO (3YR GREY FILLY)

TRAINER:	Edward Lynam
FORM:	211-
PEDIGREE:	Clodovil – Knapton Hill (Zamindar)
BHA RATING:	-
OPTIMUM TRIP:	1m

Shaped well when second on her debut at Leopardstown in July before making all to beat the very well-regarded My Titania, winner of her next two starts including a Group 3, by two and three-quarter lengths in a 6f maiden at the same track in August (hooded for the first time).

She improved again when coming from behind to beat 16 rivals in a 6f sales race at the Curragh (form only ordinary).

Half-sister to useful sprint winners Pitlochry and The Dark Wizard out of a mare that won over seven furlongs. Looks to have inherited the family's pace.

May not be up to beating the best of her generation, but trainer has done exceptionally well with horses of this type and we can be sure she will be placed to optimum effect.

VENEZIA (3YR GREY COLT)

TRAINER:	**Martyn Meade**
FORM:	**43-**
PEDIGREE:	**Galileo – St Roch (Danehill)**
BHA RATING:	-
OPTIMUM TRIP:	**1m 2f +**

Looked very much a staying type in both his starts, plugging on to finish fourth in soft ground at Sandown and then finishing well again, after becoming unbalanced, in a 1m maiden at Newmarket in October.

Fourth foal and a full brother to a winner over a mile at two. Dam is an unraced sister to US Grade 1 winner Luas Line and related to Group 2 winner Lost In The Moment.

Did not look entirely straightforward at Newmarket but has a fair share of ability and, coming from a low-profile yard, could be the sort to win a middle-distance handicap at a decent price.

WARRIOR OF LIGHT (3YR BAY COLT)

TRAINER:	**David Lanigan**
FORM:	**61-**
PEDIGREE:	**High Chaparral – Strawberry Fledge (Kingmambo)**
BHA RATING:	-
OPTIMUM TRIP:	**1m 2f**

Quickened discernibly when beating Rapid Advance by a length in a 1m maiden at Kempton in November, with a colt now rated 75 one and a quarter lengths back in third. Had shaped well when sixth on his debut at the same track in October.

Second foal out of an unraced full sister to Oaks winner Light Shift and a half-sister to Group 1 winner Shiva and 1m 4f Group 2 winner Limnos.

Runs as if he will stay beyond a mile but not necessarily bred to get much further. Has the ability to change gear.

WELD ARAB (3YR BAY COLT)

TRAINER:	Dermot Weld
FORM:	Unraced
PEDIGREE:	Shamardal – Itqaan (Danzig)
BHA RATING:	-
OPTIMUM TRIP:	7f + ?

A son of Shamardal from a top-class family.

The fourth foal of a 1m winning full sister to 1m 4f Group 3 winner and Group 1 Champion Stakes runner-up Mawatheeq and a half-sister to five winners including 1,000 Guineas and Coronation Stakes winner Ghanaati and Oaks runner-up Rumoush.

Second dam Sarayir comes from the family of Nayef, Nashwan and Unfuwain.

As well bred as anything in this book and showed his handler a fair measure of ability last season. Disappointing if he does not prove useful.

WONDERSTRUCK (3YR BAY FILLY)

TRAINER:	William Haggas
FORM:	Unraced
PEDIGREE:	Sea The Stars – Bordighera (Alysheba)
BHA RATING:	-
OPTIMUM TRIP:	1m 2f

Unraced daughter of Sea The Stars and a half-sister to eight winners including the ill-fated 2,000 Guineas winner George Washington, triple Group 1 winner Grandera, 1m 6f winner Lordofthehouse, 2m winner Old Hundred and the useful 1m 6f winner Sun Central. Dam won over 1m 5f and was Listed placed.

Bred to stay middle distances and showed her trainer enough last season to raise hopes that she will enhance her family's glowing reputation.

WRANGLER (3YR BAY COLT)

TRAINER:	William Haggas
FORM:	3-
PEDIGREE:	High Chaparral – Tipsy Me (Selkirk)
BHA RATING:	-
OPTIMUM TRIP:	1m 2f

Made a most encouraging start to his career when staying on strongly in the final quarter mile to finish a never-nearer third to Mannaro and Second Step in a 1m maiden at Yarmouth in October.

Only limited form to go on since (fifth now rated 68), but left the impression the race will turn out well.

Half-brother to a winner over seven furlongs out of a half-sister to 1m 4f Group 2 winner Plea Bargain, from the family of Group 3 winner Lay Time and Time Charter.

Looks certain to progress up through the ranks, possibly proving good enough to compete in Pattern-class company in time.

ZEE ZEELY (3YR CHESTNUT COLT)

TRAINER:	William Haggas
FORM:	52-
PEDIGREE:	Champs Elysees – Zee Zee Gee (Galileo)
BHA RATING:	-
OPTIMUM TRIP:	1m 2f +

Shaped with eye-catching promise when a strong-finishing fifth on his debut in a 7f maiden at Lingfield in October. Progressed from that next time in a 7f maiden at Newmarket, wandering and looking green entering the Dip and then picking up well to do everything but win, just held on the line by Idder.

Fourth now rated 75, beaten just over two lengths, putting the first two on a mark in the low 80s. Second foal out of an unraced half-sister to Group 1 winner Izzi Top out of Group 1 winning half-sister to Kayf Tara and Opera House.

Found the seven furlongs too sharp last season and promises to improve significantly when stepped up to a mile and a quarter or more. Sure to be placed to optimum effect by his handler.

Keep in touch

If you want to keep in touch with Marten's thoughts on a regular basis then read his free-to-view journal at:

www.martenjulian.com

or ring him on:

0906 150 1555

Selections given in the first minute

(calls charged at £1.50 a minute at all times)

Follow Marten

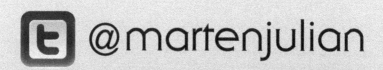 @martenjulian

THE DARK HANDICAPPERS

The following horses qualify for this section in the belief that they will start their careers in handicaps from a favourable mark.

ANJIN (3YR BAY GELDING)

TRAINER:	Sir Mark Prescott
FORM:	0-74
PEDIGREE:	Danehill Dancer – Twyla Tharp (Sadler's Wells)
BHA RATING:	-
OPTIMUM TRIP:	1m 2f +

Showed steady improvement in three runs this winter, outpaced and always behind on his racecourse debut in a 7f Class 5 maiden at Lingfield in December.

Revealed a little more next time in a similar race at Wolverhampton, pushed along in arrears and then hampered and short of room in the straight.

Put up his best run in a 1m Class 5 contest next time at Lingfield, showing up with the pace and keeping on quite well to finish fourth of eight.

Cost 110,000gns as a yearling and closely related to The Fugue and a half-brother to a winner over two miles. Dam is a 1m 1f winning half-sister to Group 1 winners Summoner and Compton Admiral.

Bred to relish middle distances and looks the right type to make steady progress up the handicap.

BILIMBI (3YR BAY GELDING)

TRAINER:	**William Haggas**
FORM:	**041-**
PEDIGREE:	**Duke Of Marmalade – Starship (Galileo)**
BHA RATING:	**82**
OPTIMUM TRIP:	**1m 2f ?**

Made giant strides in three runs last season, needing plenty of cajoling before staying on into fourth in a 7f maiden on his second start at Leicester in October.

Focused more on the job in hand next time at Yarmouth, powering away in the soft ground to beat a horse now rated 68 by four lengths, with the 4/11 favourite Istikshaf, now rated 78, a further three lengths back in third.

Full brother to 1m 2f winner Martian and related to Group 3 winner Alexander Pope out of a half-sister to the speedy Superstar Leo.

Mixed messages from the pedigree, with more speed on the distaff side than his style of racing would suggest. Stayed the seven furlongs well in testing ground at Yarmouth, so should get a mile and could get further,

May well prove better than handicap class and could not be in better hands to do so.

DUTCH RIFLE (3YR BAY FILLY)

TRAINER:	**James Tate**
FORM:	**1-**
PEDIGREE:	**Dutch Art – Vodka Shot (Holy Bull)**
BHA RATING:	**79**
OPTIMUM TRIP:	**1m 2f**

Made her debut in late December in an extended 1m maiden at Wolverhampton, and did the job in very pleasing style.

Led to post but always travelling well through the race, she took the lead on the bridle two furlongs out before quickening clear to win by just over two lengths. Runner-up won next time and the fifth, beaten here just over six lengths, is rated on 74.

Sister to a 7f winner out of a half-sister to a useful multiple winner over around a mile.

Clearly has above-average ability.

ENDLESS CREDIT (4YR BROWN GELDING)

TRAINER:	**Luca Cumani**
FORM:	**213-**
PEDIGREE:	**High Chaparral – Pay The Bank (High Top)**
BHA RATING:	**86**
OPTIMUM TRIP:	**1m 4f +**

Unraced at two but shaped like a horse with a future when winning a 1m 2f maiden at Newmarket in June.

Looked one paced next time in a 1m 2f 0-100 handicap at the same track, not given a hard time in third once beaten.

Brother to Asker, winner over 1m 6f and of a bumper and closely related to top-class staying hurdler Celestial Halo, from the family of the gutsy My Branch.

Did not race again but has been kept in training and expected to progress, especially when stepped up to a mile and a half or more.

FESTIVAL THEATRE (3YR CHESTNUT COLT)

TRAINER:	**Sir Michael Stoute**
FORM:	**41-**
PEDIGREE:	**Danehill Dancer – Scottish Stage (Selkirk)**
BHA RATING:	**85**
OPTIMUM TRIP:	**1m 2f +**

Slightly awkward individual, who steadily got the message on his debut at Salisbury before improving to win a 7f Class 5 maiden at Kempton in August.

Took a while to find his stride on both occasions, having to be switched when still behind a furlong from home at Kempton and then staying on very strongly to win snugly by a neck.

Fourth foal and a full brother to 2m hurdle winner Dumbarton (also a winner over a mile on the Flat) and closely related to 1m 4f winners Scottish Vespers and Northern Meeting. Dam won a 1m 2f Listed race and ran second in the Irish Oaks.

Just the sort you like to see in this yard and likely to be brought along steadily with a view to the long term. Found the seven furlongs too sharp at Kempton and looks sure to make significant progress when stepped up beyond a mile.

FUN MAC (3YR CHESTNUT COLT)

TRAINER:	**Hughie Morrison**
FORM:	**631-**
PEDIGREE:	**Shirocco – Favorite (Montjeu)**
BHA RATING:	**79**
OPTIMUM TRIP:	**1m 2f +**

Shaped well on his first two starts over a mile, first at Goodwood and then when finishing third in a 1m 2f maiden stakes at Pontefract. Improved again when overcoming greenness to win a 1m 2f maiden stakes at Haydock, hanging right in the closing stages but staying on well to win by two and three-quarter lengths.

Third foal and a full brother to Favorite Girl, a winner over 1m 3f.

Showed he lacked nothing in stamina to win over a mile and a quarter at two and will relish middle distances this season. Handles cut and could be a useful stayer by the autumn.

HOIST THE COLOURS (3YR BAY COLT)

TRAINER:	David Lanigan
FORM:	00-
PEDIGREE:	Sea The Stars – Multicolour Wave (Rainbow Quest)
BHA RATING:	-
OPTIMUM TRIP:	1m 4f +

Looks destined for handicaps following two not entirely unpromising runs in 1m maidens at Kempton in December.

Left a pleasing impression despite being always behind, finishing last of 13, on his debut before showing a little more, beating two of his 13 rivals, in a similar race. Not cheap at 475,000gns as a yearling and a half-brother to six winners including French Poule d'Essai des Pouliches winner Elusive Wave and other winners at around a mile. Dam, a half-sister to four winners, is out of a French Group 3 winner.

Will clearly struggle to recoup his cost but evidently being given every chance to show something through the handicap route. Requires one more run for a mark.

IMPULSIVE MOMENT (3YR CHESTNUT COLT)

TRAINER:	Andrew Balding
FORM:	51-
PEDIGREE:	Galileo – Luas Line (Danehill)
BHA RATING:	80
OPTIMUM TRIP:	1m 2f +

Would not make obvious appeal based on his half-length success in a 1m Class 5 contest on the all-weather surface at Lingfield in December, but quite well regarded by his trainer and confidently expected to improve when he is stepped up in trip.

Had been fancied to make a winning debut at Newbury in October but went into that race on the back of a rushed preparation and then found the ground softer than ideal.

Ran a little better than first impressions would suggest at Lingfield, slowly away and then a little keen and running green. Runner-up Examiner won his next two starts (now rated on 83) and fourth and fifth have also won.

By Galileo and a full brother to Ballyglasheen, a winner over hurdles and at 1m 4f on the Flat, her dam won at up to nine furlongs and is a half-sister to the stayer Lost In The Moment.

Case for arguing, through subsequent form, that he is very well treated on 80. Leaves the impression he may have a touch of class, and in good hands to exploit his mark – especially when stepped up in trip.

LAURELITA (3YR BAY FILLY)

TRAINER:	**George Baker**
FORM:	21-
PEDIGREE:	**High Chaparral – Chervil (Dansili)**
BHA RATING:	81
OPTIMUM TRIP:	1m 2f +

Beaten seven lengths by Hoku, subsequently beaten a nose in Group 3 company and now rated 98, on her debut at Windsor in August. Looked a much-improved filly when making all to win a 7f Class 5 next time at Chepstow, passing the post with more in hand than the two and a half lengths margin suggests. Runner-up a subsequent winner, now rated on 82, which casts this filly's rating in a favourable light.

Fourth foal and closely related to 1m winner Zeydan and a half-sister to a sprint winner, from the family of US Grade 1 winner Light Jig.

Bred to stay beyond a mile, and could prove very useful if she does, and from the slim evidence available she looks nicely treated on 81. Trainer likely to start her in handicaps and work on from there.

One of the more interesting horses in this section.

MAN FROM SEVILLE (4YR CHESTNUT GELDING)

TRAINER:	Sir Mark Prescott
FORM:	600/610011-
PEDIGREE:	Duke of Marmalade – Basanti (Galileo)
BHA RATING:	75
OPTIMUM TRIP:	1m 6f +

Started last season on a mark of 57 following three qualifying runs at two.

Finished sixth of seven on his seasonal return in a 1m 4f at Leicester 0-70 handicap in May before winning a 1m 6f 0-65 handicap at Redcar, off the pace and staying on very strongly close home.

Did not appear again until August, when tailed off in a 2m 0-65 handicap on soft ground at Nottingham (61). Again well beaten five weeks later at Redcar before returning to winning form stepped up to two miles in a 0-65 handicap at Lingfield, staying on strongly to win by five lengths eased down. Comfortably defied a 6lb penalty four days later at Wolverhampton, stepped up to an extended two miles.

Seemed to be improving steadily last autumn and leaves the impression he has more to offer from a mark of 75. May be one to keep in mind for a staying handicap.

Sir Mark Prescott

MANNARO (3YR BAY GELDING)

TRAINER:	Marco Botti
FORM:	1-
PEDIGREE:	Manduro – Donoma (Beat Hollow)
BHA RATING:	-
OPTIMUM TRIP:	1m 4f +

Won like a horse with more to offer when displaying a good attitude to beat two promising rivals in a 1m maiden at Yarmouth in October.

Slowly away, ducking right at the start, before switching back to the far side and enjoying a clear run thereafter. Edged ahead over a furlong out and kept finding enough to hold the determined challenge of Second Step, with the equally promising Wrangler two lengths away in third.

By Manduro and the first foal of daughter of Beat Hollow who won at Listed level over a mile and is a half-sister to some useful Italian performers between a mile and a mile and a half, from the family of an Italian St Leger winner.

Ran to a mark of around 80 on a tenuous line through the fifth. Bred to thrive over middle distances and handled the easy ground well in his maiden. Progressive sort.

MOSCATO (3YR GREY GELDING)

TRAINER:	Sir Mark Prescott
FORM:	000-
PEDIGREE:	Hernando – Alba Stella (Nashwan)
BHA RATING:	61
OPTIMUM TRIP:	1m 4f +

Ran three times over a period of 16 days in October, looking exceptionally green when last of 11 on his debut in a 1m maiden at Windsor.

Performed in a similar manner a few days later at Nottingham, pushed along vigorously from the home turn and allowed to come home in his own time.

Showed far more next time at Kempton, just off the pace until dropping back through the field in the final quarter mile.

Half-brother to four winners including 2m winner All My Heart, 1m 4f winner Aleatricis and 1m 4f winner All The Rules. Dam, a daughter of Nashwan, won over 1m 4f and is a half-sister to Alborada and Alba Nova.

Starts the season on 61 but anyone's guess how he will progress when stepped up to a trip more in accordance with his pedigree. Encouraging to see him show a little speed on his final start and looks a typical slow-burner for his canny handler.

PATENTAR (3YR BAY COLT)

TRAINER:	**Marco Botti**
FORM:	**1-**
PEDIGREE:	**Teofilo – Poppets Sweetlove (Foxhound)**
BHA RATING:	-
OPTIMUM TRIP:	**1m**

Interesting winner of a 7f Class 3 maiden at York in October, nicely backed and leading approaching the final furlong despite drifting left.

Cost 220,000gns as a yearling and a half-brother to speedy 5f winner Lady Poppy out of a 1m winning half-sister to five winners including high-class sprinter Overdose and Listed-placed Poppet's Treasure.

Has rather more speed than stamina in his family, so may not stay as far as the visual impression from York would suggest.

Has not been allocated a mark but runner-up was rated 72 at York and fourth, a winner next time, is on 78. Likely to be given a mark in the mid to high 80s as a starting point.

Hard to assess on the evidence of this one run, but impressed jockey Adam Kirby and could progress into the better handicaps or even Pattern-class contests.

PSYCHOMETRY (3YR BAY FILLY)

TRAINER:	Sir Michael Stoute
FORM:	221-
PEDIGREE:	Danehill Dancer – Seven Magicians (Silver Hawk)
BHA RATING:	81
OPTIMUM TRIP:	1m +

Did not look anything too special last season but has a staying pedigree and may improve beyond her mark when stepped up in trip.

Shaped well on her first two starts, notably on her debut in a 7f maiden at Ascot where she came with a storming late run to be beaten half a length after having to be switched for a clear run approaching the final furlong.

Did not show the same turn of foot when a fair second in a 7f maiden a month later at Newmarket. Looked a better filly on her third start in a 1m maiden at Kempton in September, coming with a run around the outside and swooping into the lead in the final furlong.

By Danehill Dancer, and a half-sister to 7f winner Magician's Cape, out of a Silver Hawk mare who won over a mile and a quarter from the family of Divine Proportions and top-class French miler Whipper.

Bred to stay beyond a mile and certainly runs as if it will suit her. Just the type to exploit her mark before moving up a grade, perhaps progressing into Pattern races.

RED PASSIFLORA (3YR BAY FILLY)

TRAINER:	**Sir Mark Prescott**
FORM:	**000-**
PEDIGREE:	**Danehill Dancer – Red Peony (Montjeu)**
BHA RATING:	**62**
OPTIMUM TRIP:	**1m 2f +**

Well-bred half-sister to three winners out of a daughter of Montjeu who won over a mile and a half.

Showed steady improvement in three runs over a five-week period in October/November, always behind in a 1m maiden at Nottingham and then a little nearer next time in a similar race at Yarmouth. Showed much more on her third start in a 1m Class 5 at Kempton, shuffled along in arrears and then making steady headway in the final quarter mile to finish a never-nearer eighth of 11, beaten just under six lengths.

Has been given every opportunity to win races from an opening mark of 62, especially when stepped up to a mile and a quarter or more.

STOMACHION (4YR BAY GELDING)

TRAINER:	**Sir Michael Stoute**
FORM:	**03511-**
PEDIGREE:	**Duke Of Marmalade – Insight**
	(Sadler's Wells)
BHA RATING:	**83**
OPTIMUM TRIP:	**1m 2f +**

Unraced at two and shaped reasonably well in his first three runs in maidens at Yarmouth, Goodwood and Wolverhampton.

Allocated a mark of 68 and stepped up to a mile and a quarter, battled bravely in the soft ground at Salisbury to just get the better of Kastini, staying on under pressure without quickening.

Stepped up again in trip, under a 6lb penalty, and ridden to make optimum use of his stamina when making all to win an extended 1m 3f 0-75 handicap at Yarmouth, eased down by four and a half lengths.

Bred to stay further, by Duke Of Marmalade out of a Sadler's Wells full sister to Irish 2,000 Guineas winner Saffron Walden. Dam was a high-class performer up to 1m 2f in France and Canada.

Was due to appear in the sales but was withdrawn and stays in training, probably in the expectation that he has more to offer.

Well suited to soft ground and will have no problem staying a mile and a half. Very likely to progress beyond his current mark (83) and could be the right type for one of the season's top staying handicaps, perhaps in the autumn when conditions should favour him. Looks tough.

THE THIRD MAN (3YR BAY COLT)

TRAINER:	**John Gosden**
FORM:	**1-**
PEDIGREE:	**Dalakhani – Spinning Queen (Spinning World)**
BHA RATING:	-
OPTIMUM TRIP:	**1m 2f**

Left the impression there was plenty more on offer when getting up close home to win a 7f maiden at Lingfield in December.

Always handy but bustled along from a wide draw, he raced a little keen and needed cajoling as the pace quickened turning for home. Found his stride and a change of gear on straightening to make up the leeway on the leader and win cosily, pulling away at the finish.

Half-brother to a handful of winners including useful 1m and 1m 2f performer Trade Commissioner and Listed middle-distance winner Gallipot out of Group 1 Sun Chariot Stakes winner Spinning Queen.

Bred to stay at least a mile and a quarter and could be more than useful if he gets further. Runner-up rated just 70, so BHA rating could be favourable.

Vallarta – can improve this season

VALLARTA (4YR BAY GELDING)

TRAINER:	**Mick Channon**
FORM:	**2631/6006322-**
PEDIGREE:	**Footstepsinthesand – Mexican Miss (Tagula)**
BHA RATING:	**76**
OPTIMUM TRIP:	**6f**

Would appear to be well exposed on the bare evidence to hand, but has run only 11 times in two seasons and there are grounds for believing he can improve this year.

Looked potentially useful when winning a Newbury maiden as a two-year-old in a quick time and confirmed that promise with two decent efforts in competitive Class 2 6f handicaps on his first two starts at three. Ran consistently thereafter without being able to take advantage of a slipping mark, having dropped from 83 to 75.

Has had remedial work over the winter and his trainer is very hopeful that he will make up for lost time.

Suited by a strongly-run six furlongs on quick ground.

WESTERN HYMN (3YR BAY COLT)

TRAINER:	John Gosden
FORM:	1-
PEDIGREE:	High Chaparral – Blue Rhapsody (Cape Cross)
BHA RATING:	-
OPTIMUM TRIP:	1m 2f + ?

Quietly impressive when coming from way off the pace to quicken through and win a 1m Class 5 maiden at Kempton on his debut last December.

Travelled well through the race and picked up nicely when switched wide for a clear run, winning by two and three-quarter lengths with plenty left in the locker. The third Roskilly rated 79, suggests the winner ran to a mark in the low 90s.

By High Chaparral and the second foal of a 7f winning half-sister to top-class Fantasia, a winner over nine furlongs in the US, from the family of Cheveley Park Stakes winner Blue Duster.

Stayed the mile well and may get further, but not certain to stay a mile and a half.

Looks just the type his trainer likes to prepare for a top handicap, and may be one to keep in mind for Royal Ascot.

THE DERBY PREVIEW

Although these are early says, as I write in mid February, the indications are that the 2014 Derby may be more about quality than quantity.

In my view a few of the colts which figure near the head of the market are uncertain to stay the trip. Furthermore, if a horse emerges this spring with what appears to be a leading chance then he may, as happened with Camelot, scare some of the others away.

Camelot started 8/13 to beat just eight rivals in his year and if **Australia**, like that colt trained by Aidan O'Brien, wins the 2,000 Guineas then you won't find the bookmakers offering much more than evens about him following up at Epsom.

Australia is just one of a clutch of likely entries from Ballydoyle, and it is possible that a lightly-raced maiden winner or two may creep into the reckoning but, at this stage, the son of Galileo stands clear market leader at 4/1 and it is not hard to see why.

Starting with his pedigree, Australia should stay the Derby trip. In fact it will be a big surprise if he doesn't because his full sister won over one and three-quarter miles – albeit from a mark of just 59 – while he has two half-brothers who won over a mile and a half.

His dam Ouija Board was, of course, a performer of the highest class at trips ranging from seven furlongs to a mile and a half.

Regarding his form Australia's best performance came in a Group 3 contest at Leopardstown.

That may not have been top drawer company but a line through third-home Kingfisher gives him the best part of a stone in hand of Royal Lodge winner Berkshire.

As for Free Eagle, the runner-up at Leopardstown, his starting price of 2/5 was based more on the high esteem in which he was held at the time by Dermot Weld than the form of his maiden four weeks earlier over the same track and trip.

Australia did enough to warrant a closing mark of 117 - just 2lb adrift of War Command – and that will provide a more than sufficient platform on which to build a high-level three-year-old campaign.

What I most liked about Australia last season was the way he matured through his races.

Green and pretty clueless when falling out of the stalls on his debut, he then beat a promising filly of Dermot Weld's named Carla Bianca before that eye-catching defeat of Free Eagle at Leopardstown.

Furthermore from a Derby perspective it was encouraging that Australia found both his stride and a gear when he was stepped up from seven furlongs to a mile.

Finally – and I appreciate this is not the first time we've heard such praise – O'Brien is on record as suggesting Australia could be the best colt he has ever trained.

Current odds of 4/1 may not appeal at such an early stage, but this colt has the profile to start a very short price at Epsom. He is, without doubt, the most exciting of this year's Derby candidates and it would not surprise me to see him prove exceptional.

It is uncertain if he will take in the 2,000 Guineas first, but if he does go to Newmarket and win – or run well – then that would be highly encouraging given that he is bred to thrive over a mile and a half.

I think we can assume that Australia is Ballydoyle's big hope for 2014.

There is unlikely to be the same sort of razzmatazz about **Kingston Hill** even though he has achieved a higher level of form.

O'Brien has a line to his ability through Oklahoma City, runner-up to him in the Autumn Stakes at Newmarket, and Johann Strauss, who was left four and a half lengths behind a fortnight later in the Racing Post Trophy.

The trainer has an even stronger line to the relative merits of the two colts though the owner, Paul Smith, who has horses at Ballydoyle along with his father Derrick Smith.

As I highlighted elsewhere there is nothing flashy about Kingston Hill but he does have a tremendous attitude. In fact in his first two runs last season he looked quite lethargic. He was, though, more focused on his work at Doncaster.

Kingston Hill is very likely to stay a mile and a half. His half-brother Ramona Chase stayed middle distances and his dam, a winner at a mile and a quarter, is related to a 1m 6f Listed and hurdle winner.

The concern is that his three runs were all on easy ground. Although his trainer says he will handle quicker going – and these days conditions never get that fast at Epsom anyway – it would be helpful to see how he copes on better ground before the big day.

O'Brien knows where he stands with Kingston Hill but if Australia doesn't make the grade then the 10/1 about Kingston Hill for Epsom would look good value.

The strange thing is his name does not appear at the first forfeit stage of the Derby entries, so obviously hold back on any bets for Epsom until we learn more.

If **Free Eagle** had not been beaten six lengths by Australia at Leopardstown in September he would possibly be near the head of the market. His trainer Dermot Weld, who knows a good horse when he sees one, was fulsome in his praise after he won his maiden at Leopardstown.

There may have been excuses for that defeat.

Ballydoyle inmate Kingfisher had finished eight lengths behind Free Eagle in his maiden but managed to close the gap to three and a half lengths when they met the next time.

Perhaps Kingfisher was improving – he ran well in the Royal Lodge Stakes on his final outing – but Free Eagle clearly needs to restore his reputation and it will be interesting to see where he is placed in the spring.

With regard to stamina, Free Eagle's half-sister stayed a mile and a half and his sire won the Derby.

Aidan O'Brien has any number of other lightly-raced colts who could make the line-up.

As we saw last year, and on past occasions, he is prepared to run more than one horse at Epsom if he thinks the race has an open look to it.

Indian Maharaja, a winner of a Listed race on his second start, was very green last season. With a dam by Danehill Dancer I would not have him as certain to stay.

Geoffrey Chaucer was the subject of favourable reports, but he may have been a little flattered when making a winning debut over a mile at Leopardstown in July as both the second and third - in a three-horse race - were ridden with a marked lack of enterprise.

He looked more convincing when he beat stable-companion Oklahoma City in the Group 2 Beresford Stakes at the Curragh, winning by a length and a quarter despite still looking green.

The plan was then to aim him at the Racing Post Trophy, but that didn't happen for a reason unknown to me.

Geoffrey Chaucer is a full brother to a winner over a mile and a half and a half-brother to five winners including the high-class Shamardal and others who stayed further. I expect him to stay middle distances.

Johann Strauss gives O'Brien a line to the top autumn form. It does not bode well in relation to Group 1 honours that the son of High Chaparral is still a maiden after three starts, but there may have been excuses for his first two defeats and it was a good effort to chase home Kingston Hill at Doncaster.

Johann Strauss is the first foal of an unraced half-sister to some useful mile and a quarter performers. Again, he should stay middle distances.

As for **War Command** he has siblings that stayed a mile and a quarter, but O'Brien spoke more than once last season about the colt's pace and it seems likely that he will be campaigned at trips up to a mile on quick ground (not entered).

One of the more interesting unexposed colts at Ballydoyle is **Blue Hussar**.

He won his only start in a 7f maiden at Leopardstown in November. The form does not add up to much, but only a good horse could have won from a position that was so far off the pace turning for home.

Behind and very green early on, he had just a couple behind him early in the straight before picking up on the outside to win cosily by three-quarters of a length.

Blue Hussar is a full brother to a winner over a mile and a half out of a daughter of Woodman related to milers. He is not certain to stay middle distances but runs as if he has sufficient stamina to do so.

It is too early to assess this colt's level but I would keep him in mind as a possible contender for a Derby, if not at Epsom then in Ireland.

The Galileo colt **Agena** got up on the line to win a 7f maiden at Leopardstown in September. His dam's side mainly comprises of horses best at trips up to a mile.

Mekong River won his first four races before finishing a 12-length fourth in the Group 1 Criterium de Saint-Cloud in November.

Illinois, winner at Tipperary of his sole start, comes into the reckoning with the runner-up winning next time and finishing fourth in a Listed race (not entered). So, too, does **Orchestra** who also won his maiden at Tipperary. **Adelaide**, a winner at Leopardstown in October, is out of a speedy mare by Elnadim so seems less likely to stay.

The unraced **Annus Mirabilis**, closely related to Ruler Of The World, is apparently well regarded at Ballydoyle. So, too, is **Horseguardsparade**, a son of Montjeu out of a daughter of Linamix.

Moving away from Ballydoyle it would seem unlikely that a colt that won his two starts over six furlongs at two should feature in a Derby preview, but as a son of Dubawi out of a mare by Galileo **Night Of Thunder** could be said to have a middle-distance pedigree.

His distaff line is actually more comprised of milers, but this colt looked rather special last season and if he stays as far as his breeding suggests he could be very good indeed (not entered).

Along the same lines it is generally assumed that **Kingman** will be campaigned over trips short of a mile and a half. As a son of Invincible Spirit out of a half-sister to Oasis Dream that would seem likely, but the colt's half-brother Remote stays a mile and a quarter. He is, though, by Dansili.

I would not discount Kingman out of hand for the Derby, but as things stand at the time of writing that target would seem unlikely. He has no entry as I write.

Keep in touch

If you want to keep in touch with Marten's thoughts on a regular basis then read his free-to-view journal at:

www.martenjulian.com

or ring him on:

0906 150 1555

Selections given in the first minute

(calls charged at £1.50 a minute at all times)

Follow Marten

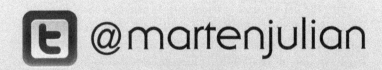 @martenjulian

Berkshire – could put Paul Cole back in the lights

Berkshire has to be a contender.

It is a while since Paul Cole had a good one, but this colt has the type of profile you used to look for in a potential Derby winner.

Promise in a good maiden, then an impressive win in the Chesham Stakes, was followed by a more hard-fought victory in the 1m Royal Lodge Stakes at Newmarket. Furthermore he has a rock-solid middle-distance pedigree and a good run in the 2,000 Guineas will set him up for Epsom.

Given there are no political considerations relating to running plans for Berkshire I would not discourage you from a modest early interest at 25/1. He acts well on quick ground.

Be Ready has something to find. He has ten-furlong blood on his distaff side but there is a lot of speed as well. I would be surprised to see him in the Derby field.

Godolphin also have **Sudden Wonder**, a son of New Approach who won his third and final start by eight lengths last October, but their colt with the stoutest pedigree is **True Story**.

The son of Manduro is out of an unraced daughter of Darshaan and following a promising opening effort behind stable-companion

Outstrip he lengthened in good style to beat a fair field in a 7f maiden at Newmarket in July.

That form worked out really well, with the second, third and fifth now rated on 99, 97 and 96 respectively. For some reason True Story did not appear again, but I will be watching out for him when he does.

Seagull Star gets favourable mention elsewhere.

As a son of Sea The Stars out of a daughter of Montjeu who stayed middle distances he looks sure to appreciate a distance of ground. He appears to have surprised connections when he won – and a mark of 81 shows what he has to find – but there was much to like about the way he did so and William Haggas will have a plan in mind for him.

Warrior Of Light, a son of High Chaparral who cost 320,000gns as a yearling, is out of an unraced full sister to Oaks winner Light Shift. He quickened well to win a 1m maiden at Kempton in November and may win races at a reasonable level.

The unraced **Hydrogen** is bred to stay. This 2,500,000gns yearling is closely related to Derby winner Authorized but it's a concern he never made it to the track last season.

John Oxx has a stoutly-bred unraced colt named **Jupiter And Mars**. As a son of Sea The Stars out of a daughter of Reference Point he could hardly be better bred for Epsom. Watch for him as the season progresses (not entered)..

Ebanoran, who narrowly landed a maiden at the Curragh in October, is likely to start in a trial. He is by Oasis Dream but has plenty of stamina on his dam's side. Stable-companion **Marakoush**, second to Century at the Curragh in October, is also bred to stay.

John Gosden's **Danjeu** is better than he showed on his sole start last season. He could be achieving a reasonable level of form by the summer (not entered). The trainer has another interesting sort in **The Third Man**, who showed a bright turn of foot to win at Lingfield before Christmas (not entered).

As mentioned elsewhere Andrew Balding trains a potentially useful sort in **Scotland**.

The son of Monsun beat a fair field over an extended mile in an Epsom maiden in September. There was talk afterwards of the Racing Post Trophy, in which I would have expected him to figure.

Scotland is the sort of horse who could run well in a trial in the spring. He will probably be competing for black type when he is stepped up beyond a mile (not entered).

Andre Fabre says he is likely to keep **Galiway** at home (not entered). **Gallante**, winner of a Longchamp maiden in September, is one for the notebook. He could be the type his trainer likes to keep for the autumn prizes.

Ectot is a high-class prospect for Elie Lellouche. The son of Hurricane Run progressed from winning an ordinary maiden at Clairefontaine in July to winning a Listed race, a Group 3 and then the Group 1 Criterium International at Saint-Cloud in November.

He is likely to stay but connections may prefer to keep him in France (not entered).

Prince Gibraltar, who came from a long way off the pace to win the Criterium de Saint-Cloud, looks sure to make an impression in top-class company. His full brother won over 1m 7f so it was not surprising he was able to win over a mile and a quarter in the mud last November (not entered).

Mikel Delzangles has a promising unraced colt named **Mystic Blue** (not entered). Look out also for **Royal Battalion**, also unraced.

Of the many other less-exposed or unraced colts **Ayrad**, **Basem**, **Dark Days**, **Emirati Spirit**, **Enzani**, **Festival Theatre**, **Katilan**, **Mahsoob**, **Rapprochement**, **Sinkal**, **Western Hymn** and **Zee Zeely** could work their way into the mix.

CONCLUSION

At the risk of being swayed by Ballydoyle's finely honed publicity machine I am happy, at this early stage, to offer my allegiance to Australia.

In a year when there were no obvious contenders for middle-distance honours, the way this colt visibly matured through racing leads me to believe that with the winter behind him he could, by June, be exceptional. Once the penny dropped, when he was asked to step up to a mile, he was very impressive and over a further half mile this summer he could be in a class of his own.

Kingston Hill is a thoroughly likeable performer – very much a 'safe pair of hands' – but he would not, at this stage, have the potential brilliance of Australia. There is also a concern that his name was missing from the first stage forfeit list.

Berkshire falls into a similar category although in his case, at 25/1, he seems overpriced given his assured stamina and proven Group-class form. Of the others I quite like Blue Hussar and True Story, while there are any number of lightly-raced maiden winners who could make an impression in an early trial.

Australia seems short enough at 4/1, but if he runs well in the Guineas that price will quickly become a distant memory. Berkshire and Kingston Hill should also make the party.

THE OAKS PREVIEW

Kazzia, back in 2002, was the last filly to land the 1,000 Guineas-Oaks double but judging by the ante-post book for the Newmarket Classic in February you would not get much of a price against this year's Oaks winner running first in the Guineas.

Contrary to the impression given by her price tag of 20/1 for Epsom, I would not necessarily assume that a mile and a half will prove beyond the current Guineas favourite **Miss France**. Whether her trainer Andre Fabre would wish to run her at Epsom is, of course, another matter.

The distaff side of her pedigree has more stamina than many of those quoted above her in the Oaks market. Her sire Dansili gets most of his top-class performers over middle distances and her dam was beaten just half a length in the 1m 4f Group 1 Prix Vermeille, having won twice over a mile at two.

Miss France is a half-sister to four winners, three of them over 1m 2f, 1m 5f and 1m 6f. One of the reasons she ran at Newmarket last autumn was for the better ground, so if she runs as well as expected in the Guineas don't be surprised to hear Andre Fabre talk of Epsom, where the going usually rides better than at Chantilly.

As you are aware from the 1,000 Guineas preview I hold out high hopes for **Balansiya**.

The daughter of Shamardal was impressive in her maiden at Leopardstown - on ground softer than her trainer Dermot Weld thought ideal – and her dam, a Group 3 winner over a mile (never raced beyond that trip), is a half-sister to 1m 4f Group 2 winner Balakheri from the family of Bering.

As Weld has already remarked on the filly's preference for quick ground this may encourage him to aim her at Epsom rather than the Curragh. A bold show in the 1,000 Guineas – should that be her target – would leave those who back her now at 33/1 on good terms with themselves.

Weld has another once-raced maiden with the potential to go places named **Tested**.

This daughter of Selkirk stayed on well to beat what turned out to be a decent field in a 7f maiden at the Curragh in September.

The form held up well, with the second, third, sixth, eighth and 16th all going on to win. Tested has a half-sister who won at 1m 6f and is out of a mare who won a Group 3 over 1m 2f from the family of a French St Leger runner-up.

After the race the trainer said that Tested would be put away for the season and should develop into a stakes filly this year. She has to be on the shortlist.

Tarfasha is a third Oaks prospect for Weld.

Following an eye-catching debut behind Geoffrey Chaucer at Leopardstown in July she showed a smart turn of foot to win a 7f maiden very easily at Galway before being put in her place by My Titania in a Group 3 at the Curragh. She is a half-sister to the useful stayer Saddler's Rock and other fair sorts, including Irish Derby runner-up Galileo Rock, so middle distances will suit her.

John Gosden's **Taghrooda** appears to have caught her connections by surprise when making a winning debut in a 1m maiden at Newmarket in September.

There was little market support for the filly, who started at 20/1, but it was evident a furlong from home that her momentum would carry her into contention. The form worked out quite well, with runner-up Casual Smile rated on 89 and the third, Tea In Transvaal, winning next time and ending the year on a mark of 79.

Taghrooda is probably a Group-class filly in the making. In fact of all the fillies in this preview she is the one most certain to appreciate middle distances. Her sire is Sea The Stars and her dam, a daughter of Sadler's Wells, won four times – three at Listed level – at trips up to 1m 6f.

Taking everything into account, Taghrooda did well to win her maiden over a mile and, in the light of her stamina-endowed pedigree, I confidently expect her to earn black type over a mile and a half. It will be very interesting to see where John Gosden starts her.

The current favourite for the Oaks is Aidan O'Brien's **Tapestry**, a daughter of Galileo but from a distaff line of horses best at up to a mile.

Following a debut victory in a 6f maiden and then a Group 2 win over seven, she was promoted from third to second after suffering interference from Kiyoshi in the Moyglare Stud Stakes. As noted in the 1,000 Guineas preview she is prone to carry her head high. There is pace on her dam's side but I would expect her to stay beyond a mile.

Marvellous, a winner for O'Brien of her sole start at Navan in October, also has a bottom line comprised of miling blood. She beat a subsequent winner, now rated on 94, with something in hand. She should also appreciate further than a mile, without being entirely certain to stay the Oaks trip.

Bracelet has a rather more complex pedigree. This daughter of Montjeu kept on pleasingly to beat Tap Dancing, with the third 12 lengths away, in a 7f maiden at Leopardstown in June. She is a full sister to 7f Group 2 winner Wading out of a dam, by Green Desert, closely related to Sea The Stars, Galileo and Black Sam Bellamy.

The presence of Green Desert in the second generation would normally impose a limitation of stamina but Bracelet stayed the seven furlongs well in her maiden and I would expect her to get at least a mile and a quarter. It would be a concern that she was not seen out again after June.

Dazzling, a full sister to Irish 2,000 Guineas winner Roderic O'Connor, needs to improve. An encouraging start in a 1m maiden at the Curragh in September was followed by fair runs in two Listed races. She did not look the strongest of finishers last season.

Shell House, second to Dazzling at the Curragh, subsequently ran sixth in a 7f maiden at Leopardstown. She is out of a mare by Dayjur and has little prospect of staying the Oaks trip.

My Titania, trained by John Oxx, was all out to beat the 86-rated Chicago Girl on her third and final start at the Curragh. That filly was beaten in a Listed race next time out, which leaves this daughter of Sea The Stars with plenty to find. She is, though, likely to improve when racing beyond a mile and last autumn her trainer mentioned the Oaks as a possible target.

Ihtimal, by Shamardal from the family of Oaks and Irish Derby winner Balanchine, showed steady improvement last autumn. She ended her campaign with a creditable third in the Fillies' Mile and returned in February better than ever when winning the UAE 1,000 Guineas at Meydan and three weeks later the UAE Oaks by 10 lengths. She is expected to have taken her chance against the colts in the UAE Derby at the end of March by the time you read this.

Godolphin will have others to call upon by June but this progressive filly has every chance of staying the trip without being certain to do so.

I am less sure about the stamina of **Amazing Maria**.

Her dam won over six furlongs and did not appear to stay much further and this filly had a keen way of racing last year. I would not view as her as an Oaks candidate at this stage.

Charlie Hills has a strong team of three-year-olds and one of his most interesting is **Cambridge**, a daughter of Rail Link out of a mare by Selkirk that won the Cheshire Oaks. The filly overcame obvious signs of inexperience when staying on from a few lengths off the pace to beat Regardez by three-quarters of a length over an extended mile at Nottingham in October.

The second, who won next time, is rated on 82 but the fourth was subsequently beaten and is now on a mark of 67. Cambridge stayed the mile well on her debut and should get further, but she needs to run well in a trial to warrant an Oaks target.

Volume was going the right way for Luca Cumani last autumn. The daughter of Mount Nelson confirmed the promise shown in third on her debut at Newmarket in August when easily landing a 1m maiden a month later at Newcastle.

The following month she went to Nottingham for a 1m 1f nursery where, rated on 80, she battled bravely to beat the 85-rated Gold Trail by a length and a quarter, with the third three and a half lengths away.

She was subsequently raised 6lb to 86, which could still look a good mark if handicaps are the way her trainer wants to go. As a daughter of Mount Nelson out of a half-sister to a St Leger runner-up from the family of a Prix Cadran winner, Volume looks sure to appreciate a step up in trip.

Volume does not have the profile one would expect from a

potential Oaks winner but she displayed a gutsy attitude last season and looks sure to stay. One possible concern in relation to Epsom is that she shows a slight knee action.

Joyeuse, a half-sister to Frankel and Group 3 winners Bullet Train and Noble Mission, never ran beyond six furlongs last season. She was not beaten far on her final start in the Cheveley Park Stakes but her style of racing and pedigree suggest she is unlikely to be tried at a mile and a half.

CONCLUSION

It will pay to take careful note of Andre Fabre's early statements on the programme for Miss France. From my way of reading her pedigree she has every chance of staying the trip and her liking for good ground could sway them towards Epsom.

Dermot Weld holds a strong hand, with Balansiya his most exciting prospect. John Oxx has already mentioned the Oaks as a possible target for My Titania, while Aidan O'Brien can call upon a number of lightly-raced fillies, with Tapestry the most obvious.

I am very keen on Taghrooda and I will be keeping a close eye on her early target, in the hope that it is one of the established trials. I also like Volume, who will be brought along patiently by her talented handler.

The two which interest me, at 33/1 as I write, are Balansiya and Taghrooda.

Keep in touch

If you want to keep in touch with Marten's thoughts on a regular basis then read his free-to-view journal at:

www.martenjulian.com

or ring him on:

0906 150 1555

Selections given in the first minute

(calls charged at £1.50 a minute at all times)

Follow Marten

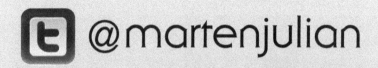 @martenjulian

THE 1,000 GUINEAS PREVIEW

You never know for certain how these things will turn out but, writing in February, this year's 1,000 Guineas promises to be a decent renewal, with a field comprising a strong representation from France, a couple of relatively unexposed fillies from Ireland and rock-solid Group form from the home team.

The market is headed at 11/2 by Andre Fabre's **Miss France**, a daughter of Dansili and the ninth living foal of 1m Group 1 winner Miss Tahiti, who won the Prix Marcel Boussac at two but failed to win again despite being placed three times in Group 1 company.

There was precious little encouragement from this filly's racecourse debut, when she finished ninth of 10 in a 6f maiden at Deauville in August. Later that month and stepped up to a mile she was seen in a far better light, racing keenly in the early stages and then quickening entering the final furlong to beat subsequent Prix Marcel Boussac winner Indonesienne by one and a quarter lengths (the fourth Xcellence also won next time out).

Miss France – a filly of great talent

It is very rare for Andre Fabre to bring a two-year-old over to England, so it was no surprise to see her attract strong market interest when she lined up for the Group 3 Oh So Sharp Stakes just less than a month later at Newmarket.

Racing on the fastest ground she had tackled, and back in trip, the concern was that things were going to happen too quickly for her. Despite the strong pace she again raced keenly in the early stages before making smooth headway two furlongs from home under Mickael Barzalona.

Devouring the ground, she maintained her momentum to lead inside the final furlong and hold Lightning Thunder by a head, winning with more in hand than the margin suggests. The time was reasonable given that they were racing into a strong headwind.

Miss France left the strong impression that seven furlongs was her minimum requirement. Having already shown good form over a mile, there need be no concerns about the Guineas trip. She also appears to be blessed with a fine turn of foot and, unlike most horses trained in France, she evidently handles quicker ground.

The concern is that the form of the race did not work out at all well. Runner-up Lightning Thunder started 8/11 next time out for the Group 2 Rockfel Stakes but could finish only fourth. The fifth, Stealth Missile, was afterwards beaten 45 lengths in Listed company.

By contrast the form of her earlier race, at Chantilly in August, could not have worked out better.

Miss France's distaff pedigree is not short of stamina. Four of her siblings won at trips ranging from 1m 2f to 1m 6f while her sire, Dansili, gets winners over middle distances. Indeed, assuming that she learns to settle, I would not discount Miss France's prospects of staying the Oaks trip.

Of the runners in this year's 1,000 Guineas, Miss France is the one most likely to be powering up the hill. The ground seems immaterial to her and stamina won't be an issue. The only slight worry is whether her form is good enough.

Aidan O'Brien's most obvious contender is **Tapestry**, a daughter of Galileo out of Moyglare Stud Stakes and Prix Marcel Boussac

Tapestry – may be best beyond a mile

winner Rumplestiltskin. A sister to two winners in Why and the ill-fated but highly regarded Theatre, her dam side traces back to the family of Miesque.

They don't come much better bred than this, and so connections would have been pleased to win a 6f maiden at the Curragh in July and then a Group 2 race over seven furlongs at the same track the following month.

Tapestry tackled the Group 1 Moyglare Stud Stakes on her final outing, starting a strongly supported 2/1 second favourite to beat the more proven Rizeena and Kiyoshi. Things did not run smoothly for her in the race, as she was hampered twice by the eventual second Kiyoshi and came home a head behind that filly in third.

The stewards reversed placings with the second in a subsequent enquiry but my impression was that Rizeena would have won regardless of the interference.

Furthermore Tapestry, who gallops with a high head carriage, looks more a staying type than a filly with gears, so I would not expect the best to be seen of her until she is asked to tackle trips of a mile and a quarter or more.

Rizeena sets the benchmark for this year's Guineas.

There was word from an early stage of last season that the daughter of Iffraaj was useful, and following a promising debut at Newmarket in April she won a 5f maiden at Ascot in May. Almost three weeks later she made all to win the Listed National Stakes at Sandown by three lengths.

She then went to Ascot for the Queen Mary Stakes where, despite forfeiting ground by hanging right, she pulled away to win by two lengths. She had no answer to Lucky Kristale's turn of foot in the Duchess of Cambridge Stakes before running her best race five weeks later against the colts in the Prix Morny at Deauville, coming with a strong late flourish to finish third to No Nay Never and Vorda.

Stepped up to seven furlongs next time for the Group 1 Moyglare Stud Stakes, Rizeena again produced a strong late run to beat Kiyoshi (subsequently demoted to third) and Tapestry.

Rizeena was unable to contain the late burst of the ill-fated Chriselliam on her final start in the Group 1 Fillies' Mile, but it would have taken a superstar to beat that winner in the form she was in last autumn. Having said that, Rizeena's performance did not suggest she was entirely suited by the step up to a mile.

Rizeena – a wonderfully tough and consistent filly

That now looks pretty good form, with third-home Ihtimal subsequently doing well out at Meydan.

There is much to admire about Rizeena. She is very consistent, very tough and versatile regarding trip and ground. Having said that, she raced eight times last season and one is entitled to wonder if others may have the greater scope for improvement. From a personal point of view there is also a concern about her staying the mile.

I have an inkling that she may prove best at a little short of that trip but it would not surprise me to see Rizeena go very close in the Guineas and, at 10/1 as I write in February, I suggest that she is marginally overpriced.

That view has to be tempered by the fact she is also entered for the 2,000 Guineas. That would be an ambitious option but, given the trainer's optimistic approach to campaigning his horses, if the colts' Classic looked weak he may elect to make the switch.

Lucky Kristale brings admirable credentials into the mix but, in her case, I am confident that she will not stay a mile.

Her sire Lucky Story gets winners over middle distances but her dam is by Pivotal and her two previous foals won at five and six furlongs respectively.

Lucky Kristale might have ended the season unbeaten had trainer George Margarson not, in his own words, left her "undercooked" for the Albany Stakes at Royal Ascot, in which she finished sixth.

She showed a great attitude right from the start, putting her head down and battling to beat Our Queenie by a short head in a 6f maiden auction race at Newmarket. A fortnight later she won a 6f novice stakes at Yarmouth before going for the Albany Stakes, for which she was more strongly fancied than her 20/1 starting price suggests.

She vindicated her trainer's view that she had not been at her best at Ascot when quickening from off the pace to beat Rizeena comfortably by two and a quarter lengths in the Group 2 Duke of Cambridge Stakes at Newmarket. The following month she again quickened to beat Queen Catrine in the Group 2 Lowther Stakes at York.

Lucky Kristale – may be best short of a mile

Afterwards the trainer said that despite her success he felt the filly was still not "spot on" for the race. The intention was then to tackle the Cheveley Park but she scoped dirty and her blood was found to be wrong, so she was retired for the season.

Tom Queally believes the filly will stay seven furlongs and, probably, a mile but despite her relaxed way of racing her pedigree suggests otherwise.

John Oxx is seldom far adrift in his assessment of a horse's ability and he holds out high hopes for **My Titania**.

The daughter of Sea The Stars, also trained by Oxx, confirmed the promise shown on her debut in a 6f maiden at Leopardstown in August when returning to the track and staying on strongly to win what turned out to be a fairly ordinary 7f maiden by two and a quarter lengths.

Three weeks later she again galloped on resolutely to beat Chicago Girl by half a length in a Group 3 race at the Curragh.

My Titania does not appear to have the turn of foot of Miss France, but one could argue that she is not bred to. Her sire Sea The Stars seems to be passing on more stamina than speed to his progeny, while her dam is by Danehill and closely related to middle-distance winners.

The trainer says the filly may take her chance in both the 1,000 Guineas and the Oaks. The Newmarket Classic has proved a sound guide to Epsom over the years and there is a case for having an early interest at 12/1.

At this stage I would be surprised if My Titania has the pace to win the 1,000 Guineas. Also her form falls way short of the required standard. She is, though, in the perfect hands to improve and I foresee her staying on at the finish, and that would be as good an Epsom trial as you could wish for.

Amazing Maria is entitled to consideration.

Following promising runs in Class 4 maidens at Newbury, the first over seven furlongs and the second over six, she ran out an impressive six-lengths winner of a 7f Class 2 maiden at Goodwood. The form did not work out particularly well – the third Jersey Brown is currently rated on 63 – but she stepped up again over the same course and distance in the Group 3 Prestige Stakes just over three weeks later, making all to beat Qawaasem by two and a half lengths in a decent time.

Amazing Maria was improving at quite a rate last autumn and her pedigree and style of racing suggest she should stay a mile, but not much further. A line through Prestige fourth Midnite Angel leaves her about 10lb adrift of Miss France, but there is probably improvement to come and she has done more than enough to warrant a crack at the Guineas.

Visually the most impressive performance I saw from a juvenile filly last year – excepting the late Chriselliam's breathtaking victory at Santa Anita – came from **Kiyoshi** in the Albany Stakes at Royal Ascot.

The margin would have been even greater had she not hung right, while the form held up to the closest inspection with the likes of Sandiva, Joyeuse, Wedding Ring, Lucky Kristale and Wonderfully subsequently going on to win or run well at a high level.

Kiyoshi's tendency to hang cost her second place next time in the Moyglare Stud Stakes at the Curragh, where she knocked Tapestry off her stride in the final 100 yards. Her connections were a little disappointed when she finished third on her final start in the Cheveley Park Stakes, suggesting afterwards that the ground was faster than ideal and the six-furlong trip an inadequate test.

Kiyoshi looked very special on the day she won the Albany, and in fairness there was no disgrace in her two subsequent runs. Her pedigree indicates that a mile should fall within her range. Her dam won at a mile and a quarter and stayed further even though she is closely related to useful sprinters Ya Malak and Dominica. Kiyoshi has a half-brother who has won over hurdles.

There are lines of form which leave Kiyoshi a few pounds adrift of the best, but if she stays a mile and can reproduce the brilliance we saw from her at Royal Ascot then she could prove the main line of defence against the French.

Indonesienne gave Miss France's Chantilly form a timely boost when coming with a long sweeping run from off the pace to win the Group 1 Prix Marcel Boussac by three-quarters of a length from Lesstalk In Paris, with Queen Catrine a further one and three-quarter lengths back in third.

A line through Queen Catrine gives the winner a slight edge over Lucky Kristale, although given the contrasting circumstances – six furlongs on quick ground at York as opposed to a mile on soft ground at Longchamp – the line is probably tenuous.

Indonesienne stayed the mile really well at Longchamp, as her pedigree suggested she would. She is a half-sister to three winners at a mile or more out of a mare by Darshaan who is a sister to a middle-distance winner. Her sire Muhtathir was a top miler who gets winners over middle distances.

I see no reason why Indonesienne should not stay a mile and a half. She does, though, have a pedigree strongly predisposed to give in the ground and there is no indication yet that she will travel over to Britain for the Classics. Her trainer Christophe Ferland may be unwilling to tackle Miss France again, preferring to stay at home for the French options (not entered).

Vorda gave another boost to the French form when coming with a strong run from off the pace to beat Princess Noor in the Cheveley Park Stakes in September.

Vorda – not sure to stay a mile

The daughter of Orpen won her first three races – including a Listed contest and a Group 2 – before running second to No Nay Never, with Rizeena three-quarters of a length back in third, in the Prix Morny.

After the race trainer Philippe Sogorb spoke in glowing terms about the filly, adding as a cautionary note that she had a lot of speed and was not sure to stay the mile.

That may well have proved to be the case when she went to Santa Anita for the Breeders' Cup Juvenile Fillies Turf, where she started to make headway three furlongs out before her run petered out in the final quarter mile.

Vorda is the second foal of her dam, a dual winner over five furlongs. The first foal, a full sister to Vorda, was also a winner over five furlongs.

Vorda looks as if she will stay seven furlongs but I will be surprised if she gets a mile, especially at Newmarket.

Freddie Head is probably keen to keep **Royalmania** at home. The daughter of Elusive Quality won her first two starts at Deauville and Chantilly before running fourth to Indonesienne at Longchamp (not entered).

John Gosden – another strong team

Dorothy B, beaten two and a half lengths in the Cheveley Park, is one to consider.

The daughter of Fastnet Rock overcame greenness to beat Hoku – now rated on 98 – in a 6f maiden at Nottingham in August. Just over a month later she finished like a train when just failing to catch Joyeuse in the 6f Listed Dick Poole Stakes at Salisbury, looking as if she were crying out for a stiffer test.

John Gosden then stepped her up in grade for the Group 1 Cheveley Park Stakes. Probably mindful that she needed further,

William Buick gave her a very positive ride from the front. Showing good pace, she was still leading entering the dip and kept on well to finish just over two lengths away in fifth.

Dorothy B is a half-sister to a winner over 1m 2f out of a twice-raced half-sister to a Group 3 winner over a mile and a half. Although her sire is an influence for speed, Dorothy B's style of racing bodes well for a step up to a mile.

At this stage the filly has a few pounds to find, but that may well be possible when she is asked to tackle a longer trip.

As you know I am also very keen on Newmarket maiden winner **Taghrooda**. The daughter of Sea The Stars has a pedigree chock-full of stamina, but if she were to run well here that would be most encouraging for the Oaks.

The most impressive winner of a fillies' maiden race I saw anywhere last season was **Balansiya** when she beat Upper Silesian by seven lengths over 7f at Leopardstown in November.

The daughter of Shamardal moved effortlessly into the lead a quarter of a mile out before drawing clear to win eased down. It was too late in the season to assess the value of the form but the way she lengthened away, without coming off the bridle, was quite breathtaking. Afterwards Dermot Weld suggested the soft ground would not have been ideal for her, a view borne out by her pedigree. Regarding her trip, she is the first foal of a daughter of Dalakhani who won a 7f maiden at two and then a Group 3 over a mile at three.

It is exciting to ponder the prospect that Balansiya may be even better on quicker ground. Much will depend on how she does in the spring, but on the evidence from that day in November she could be heading for great heights.

Weld has another string to his bow with the twice-raced maiden **Carla Bianca**.

The grey daughter of Dansili shaped well when running Australia to three-quarters of a length on her debut in a 7f maiden at the Curragh in July. She was then asked to take a major step up in class for the Group 1 Moyglare Stud Stakes and belied her odds with a most encouraging effort, staying on under hands and heels to finish just over four lengths behind Rizeena in fourth.

Carla Bianca did well to show such useful form over seven furlongs because her pedigree is all about stamina. Her dam, a daughter of Linamix, is an unraced half-sister to 1m 6f winner Profound Beauty from the family of a Ribblesdale Stakes winner.

Expect to see this interesting prospect come into her own over a mile and a half (not entered).

Aidan O'Brien is sure to have a few promising fillies waiting in the wings if Tapestry falls short.

Dazzling, a winner of a 1m maiden at the Curragh on her debut, shaped well in Listed company on her next two starts. She is bred for further than a mile (not entered).

Marvellous beat a subsequent winner when taking a 1m Navan maiden on her only start in October. She is by Galileo out of a full sister to Giant's Causeway.

Ihtimal ran against the best of her generation last season and returned this winter in great form, winning the UAE 1,000 Guineas by three and a quarter lengths. She finished two lengths behind Rizeena when they were second and third in the Fillies' Mile having won the Sweet Solera Stakes and the May Hill earlier in the season.

Ihtimal – has done great things at Meydan

There is not much of her but she is evidently in good shape after her winter break.

Sir Michael Stoute's **Radiator** ran out a hugely impressive 15-lengths winner of a 7f maiden at Lingfield on her second start but she was then put in her place by Miss France in the Oh So Sharp Stakes at Newmarket. The daughter of Dubawi comes from the family of Banks Hill and other high-class performers. She is probably better than she looked at Newmarket.

Sandiva, who won three of her first four starts and ran second to Kiyoshi at Royal Ascot, ended her season with a fair seventh in the Prix Marcel Boussac. She is entitled to take her chance.

Al Thakira caught the eye when making a winning debut at Yarmouth in September and then four weeks later in the Group 2 Rockfel Stakes at Newmarket. Connections were concerned about the seven furlongs, with some justification as her dam is by Green Desert, but there was no sign of her stopping as she drew clear to beat Blockade by just over three lengths.

She then went to Santa Anita for the Breeders' Cup Juvenile Fillies' Turf but ran keen and finished last, possibly not suited to the fast ground or the mile.

Marco Botti may want to see how the filly gets on in a trial, but at this stage I would not be expecting her to stay a mile.

Others to consider are **Betimes**, **Bracelet**, **Folk Melody**, **Hadaatha** and **Lady Heidi**.

CONCLUSION

Miss France has plenty going for her. Andre Fabre would not have brought her over to Newmarket last autumn unless he had the 1,000 Guineas in mind.

Rizeena has the form in the book but, after a busy season, she may not have as much scope for improvement as Miss France. There is also that nagging doubt about her over a mile and her target.

My Titania has something to prove but John Oxx is seldom far adrift in his judgement and he mentioned this race as a possible target after she won.

Dorothy B could creep into the picture. She has had a good winter and the step up to a mile may bring about the few pounds of improvement needed for her to figure.

The two I like most, at this stage, are Kiyoshi and Balansiya. It would be fitting if Charlie Hills were to train the winner following his misfortune with Chriselliam and his narrow defeat with Just The Judge here last year.

Kiyoshi looked very special in the Albany and the trip should be fine.

Balansiya is far less exposed and is not certain to run, but whatever the programme I confidently expect her to take high rank.

THE 2,000 GUINEAS PREVIEW

It was disappointing that we did not see **Kingman** take his chance in one of the top juvenile contests last autumn – a chip in a joint required surgery – but he did more than enough in his two appearances to warrant his current position, as I write in mid-February, at the head of the ante-post market.

The post-race comments of trainer John Gosden suggest his debut victory in a 7f Class 4 maiden at Newmarket in June did not come as a great surprise. However the manner of it may have done.

Steadily away, losing a length or two at the gate, he was gently cajoled along at halfway with the look of a horse that was going to stay on steadily and finish in mid-division. Yet once he was switched left to get a clear run, about a quarter of a mile from home, he went into the lead and powered away to beat Adhwaa by six lengths.

The time of the race was good and the form held up well. Runner-up Adhwaa won next time out and ended the season with a rating of 92, finishing second in a Listed race on the Rowley Mile in November. The third Sea The Skies won next time at Sandown while a few of those further back also shaped well in their subsequent starts.

Priced at 16/1 for the Guineas after that race, Kingman's odds shortened following favourable analysis and comment in the trade press, with the result that there was high expectation when he appeared two months later in the Solario Stakes.

Starting at 2/7, he travelled comfortably last of the four runners before moving up alongside the leader a quarter of a mile out. Nudged along for a few strides by James Doyle, as he had been at Newmarket, he then found a change of gear to pull a couple of lengths clear of the 100-rated Emirates Flyer, with 105-rated Music Theory a further head away in third.

Afterwards Doyle said it had been a "messy race", having not gone very fast early on. In that respect it was encouraging how well the colt settled.

Kingman's pedigree is that of a miler. A son of Invincible Spirit, he is the seventh foal of French 1,000 Guineas winner Zenda, who is a half-sister to the top-class sprinter Oasis Dream from the family of Irish Oaks winner Wemyss Bight.

Kingman is a half-brother to last year's highly progressive Royal Ascot winner Remote and Panzanella, a winner over seven furlongs.

The form of the Solario Stakes received a boost when runner-up Emirates Flyer won the UAE 2,000 Guineas Trial at Meydan and then finished second to Long John in the UAE 2,000 Guineas itself.

The plan was then to aim Kingman at either the Dewhurst or the Prix Jean-Luc Lagardere at Longchamp, but a report came through in late October that the colt had undergone minor surgery to remove a chip in his joint. There were also rumours after the turn of the year that the colt could miss the season, but these were denied by John Gosden.

We do not really know too much about Kingman at this stage.

From the little we have seen of him I would say he is a horse that lengthens rather than quickens. That was certainly the case on his debut and, to a lesser extent, next time at Sandown.

Regarding his optimum trip I would not expect him to stay much beyond a mile. There is stamina on his distaff side but there is also, through Oasis Dream, a great deal of speed. Indeed, there is a case for suggesting that a stiff mile could find him out. However his relaxed way of racing makes that unlikely.

In relation to his going requirements Kingman enjoyed the good to firm going at Sandown and his sire's progeny are strongly predisposed to fast ground.

Kingman remains a colt of great potential rather than one that is proven. The setback last autumn would be a concern, as could soft ground, but in an open race it is right that he heads the market.

As expected Aidan O'Brien has a strong representation, headed by Australia and War Command.

Every season a Ballydoyle colt seems to be picked out by his trainer for special praise and, in fairness, more often than not the one that is chosen goes on to take high rank.

Last year's subject of special mention was **Australia**, a 525,000gns son of Galileo out of the outstanding Ouija Board.

Horses with such illustrious breeding seldom live up to their pedigrees, but by the end of the season Australia had done enough to establish himself as the best of his dam's progeny to date.

His debut came in a 7f maiden at the Curragh in June.

Losing a few lengths at the gate, he ran green before starting to pick up two furlongs from home. Everything then seemed to fall into place and he finished with a flourish, failing by a fast-diminishing quarter of a length to catch Renaissance Art, who didn't run again.

Three weeks later Australia returned to the Curragh for a similar race, starting 30/100 as much on the strength of his reputation as the promise shown on his debut.

This time he started on equal terms and was soon travelling nicely just off the pace. Leading two furlongs out he comfortably held the late challenge of Carla Bianca, a promising filly trained by Dermot Weld.

That turned out to be better form than it looked at the time, with the runner-up running a very creditable fourth to Rizeena next time out in the Group 1 Moyglare Stud Stakes.

Afterwards O'Brien confirmed the impression that the colt was not a quick learner.

"Australia fell asleep in the stalls last time and was still very babyish today. The penny hasn't dropped for him yet but he could be anything and we'll take our time with him."

At this stage Australia was no more than a promising winner of a maiden, albeit an immature one with more than a little potential.

Australia – could be a superstar

Next time out he appeared in 1m Group 3 contest at Leopardstown, pitched in against Dermot Weld's very well regarded maiden winner Free Eagle.

It is not often that a highly vaunted Ballydoyle colt plays second fiddle in the market to a horse from another yard, but such was the high esteem in which Free Eagle was held that he started 2/5 to win the race, with Australia at 5/2.

Just as on his debut Australia was sluggish out of the stalls but was soon back on the bridle, running a little freely before settling on the turn for home. Produced to challenge two furlongs from home, Australia found an immediate change of gear to pull six lengths clear of Free Eagle, with another Ballydoyle inmate Kingfisher a further three and a half lengths back in third.

A line through the third – officially rated 99 after running a fair race next time in the Royal Lodge Stakes at Newmarket – suggests there was no fluke about the result.

Free Eagle probably ran to a mark of around 108, which would put Australia a pound or two above his closing BHA rating of 117. The race was run in a good time and afterwards the trainer said:

"We have always thought there was something rather different about him. We really have always thought the world of him. He doesn't know he is a racehorse yet. He is very special and it was good experience for him today as he had to come round and pass horses.

"Everyone knows we always thought he was the best horse we've ever had. He lost three or four lengths in the stalls the first day and the next day was very green. I don't want to be blowing up the horse but he was always doing things no two-year-old has ever done before. He is something you dream of."

The colt's pedigree suggests that he was entitled to benefit from the extra furlong.

His full sister Filia Regina has, to date, run just five times and showed her best form when stepped up to a mile and three-quarters for a low-grade handicap at Yarmouth. Her half-brothers Voodoo Prince and Aegaeus won races over middle distances, while Ouija Board was a seven-race Grade/Group 1 winner at trips up to a mile and a half.

I would be very surprised if Australia did not stay a mile and a half and a bold display in the 2,000 Guineas, if that is his target, will probably see him promoted to clear favouritism for the Derby.

What was so pleasing about his form last season was the manner in which he progressed from race to race. He certainly looked the part on his final outing.

You can never be sure how the balls will be juggled, but I think we can safely assume Australia is Ballydoyle's big hope for the Classics.

War Command has superior form to Australia despite having a BHA rating just 2lb higher. A strong and powerfully built individual, he got up in the last strides to beat Intensified in a 7f maiden on his debut at Leopardstown in June.

Just 11 days later he appeared in the Coventry Stakes, starting 20/1 behind stable-companions Stubbs, the 5/2 favourite, and Sir John Hawkins (6/1).

Held up in last by Seamie Heffernan on the nearside of the group, a forward move two furlongs out carried him through with such momentum that he had pulled six lengths clear by the line.

Afterwards O'Brien said the horse was all about "speed and fast ground" – something to bear in mind in relation to the Guineas.

Just less than two months later he went to the Curragh for the Group 1 Phoenix Stakes, for which he started 2/5. Held up last of the five runners, he was being shuffled along by Joseph O'Brien

War Command – best on quick ground this summer

before halfway and the turn of foot that had been so evident at Royal Ascot never materialised, as he came home well held in third.

It was a surprise to see him appear again just 13 days later, when he stepped up to seven furlongs for the Group 2 Futurity Stakes at the Curragh. Once again he needed cajoling at halfway but on this occasion he picked up well, drawing three lengths clear of a fair horse in second.

After the race O'Brien said the colt may not have been primed for the Phoenix Stakes, having had a break after Royal Ascot, adding that he got the seven furlongs well.

The plan had been to run him in the National Stakes but instead he went to Newmarket for the Dewhurst, encountering easy ground for the first time.

Starting a shade of odds-on at 10/11, he seemed to travel better than in the past but again required firm driving to take the lead and hold the late challenge of Cable Bay. It was a workmanlike performance.

Afterwards O'Brien confirmed that he had been very worried about the ground, adding that the colt had a "beautiful action" and that he really required quicker conditions, as had been the case when he won at Ascot.

Both trainer and jockey seem fairly sure the colt will stay a mile this season, a view endorsed by his pedigree. His full brother Warbird won over a mile and a quarter in France and he has other siblings with winning form over a mile or more. The dam won over a mile and a quarter.

War Command is tough and may have been a little unfortunate not to end the season unbeaten. He does not, though, travel as well as Australia and unlike that colt has little prospects of staying beyond a mile.

For all his talent – and, as a Group 1 winner, he has accomplished more than Australia – War Command does not seem to have his stable companion's turn of foot. Also, he does not appear to be held in quite the same high regard by his trainer.

It would not surprise me to see War Command reach his peak over seven furlongs or a mile on the quicker summer ground.

Indian Maharaja, a son of Galileo and the first foal of Irish 1,000 Guineas winner Again, shaped with great promise when winning at Gowran Park and then followed up in a Listed race at Tipperary in August (not entered).

The colt has already won over a mile and is beautifully bred, but his form did not work out well and he has plenty still to prove.

There was a lot of talk about **Great White Eagle** before he made a successful debut at Naas in August. Just under a month later he won a 6f Group 3 at the Curragh before disappointing when 2/1 favourite in the Middle Park Stakes. He is related to horses best at trips up to a mile. An early trial will show connections the way to go (not entered).

Carlo Bugatti, a winner at Galway in September, is worth noting (not entered) while Breeders' Cup Juvenile Turf runner-up **Giovanni Boldini** had a progressive profile, progressing from a Dundalk minor race in September to that fine effort at Santa Anita.

If you want a horse to follow in the top races this season then you could do worse than side with **Kingston Hill**, an admirably game colt trained by Roger Varian.

The one caveat is that we have not yet seen him race on ground quicker than good to soft but, that apart, this tenacious performer has plenty going for him.

It all started in a 7f maiden at Newbury in September where he stayed on strongly in the closing stages to edge out the 4/6 favourite Exchequer.

The following month he was raised in class for the Group 3 Autumn Stakes at Newmarket. Settled in the early stages, he was tucked in on the nearside rail but looked in trouble at halfway, struggling to pick up as the pace quickened.

Responding bravely to his rider's urgings he managed to weave his way through to come with a late challenge and outstay Oklahoma City, who a week earlier had beaten Postponed in a valuable sales race at the same course.

Afterwards the trainer said that Kingston Hill was a "good-moving colt" who would be fine on better ground, adding that the colt was very "laid back" and would get further.

A fortnight later Kingston Hill was sent to Doncaster for the Group 1 Racing Post Trophy.

Racing handier than at Newmarket, settled about three lengths off the lead in fourth, he again needed to be shaken up when the pace quickened. It was the best part of a furlong before he started to respond to Andrea Atzeni's urgings but once he found his stride he started to pull away to beat Johann Strauss by four and a half lengths.

Afterwards the trainer said:

"Kingston Hill is a beautiful mover and next year will be an open book. He has a great cruising speed and turn of foot, so you would not rule out the Guineas."

I am not sure the evidence supports Varian's views.

Kingston Hill has never travelled that well through his races and, to my eyes, appears to lengthen rather than quicken. Furthermore he is unproven on quicker ground.

This is no surprise in the light of the colt's pedigree as he is a half-brother to Ramona Chase, a middle-distance winner, out of a daughter of Rainbow Quest related to 1m6f Listed winner and useful hurdler Lord Jim.

Varian has already said that if the colt runs at Newmarket he will not have a race beforehand.

"We would like to start him in the 2,000 Guineas but it's a blank canvas. His homework towards the end of March will tell us a lot. If he doesn't show enough zip he will go for a Derby trial but my

Kingston Hill – most impressive at Doncaster

expectation is that it will be Newmarket. A 2,000 Guineas on fast ground would be a different dynamic to what he has experienced, but I am very confident he will be just as effective on it."

I have a great fondness and respect for this colt. He is not flashy, and can look rather awkward, but he digs deep and finds. This may be because he is not a natural miler and, to my eyes, everything about him points to his appreciating middle distances.

Indeed, looking to the longer term, I could see him developing into a St Leger candidate.

Kingston Hill may not have the allure of a few of the colts around this year, but he is thoroughly genuine and is the type who will never let you down. That is as much as you can ask of any horse.

Things have gone very well for Middleham Park Racing in the last few years and they have something rather special on their hands with **Toormore**.

The son of Arakan showed a good attitude for a debutant when overcoming a wide draw and coming away with Ertijaal to win an above-average Class 4 maiden at Leicester in May. That form was made to look pretty good when the runner-up, now rated on 98, hacked up by six lengths a month later in June.

Toormore was then sent to Goodwood for the Group 2 Vintage Stakes, where he was up against impressive Newmarket maiden winner Outstrip and Coventry Stakes runner-up Parbold.

Settled and tucked in on the rails, he looked in trouble as the pace quickened a quarter of a mile from home before staying on late to catch Outstrip in the closing strides.

This was not an overly impressive performance to the eye, but both Richard Hannon Jnr and jockey Richard Hughes stressed afterwards that the colt was still "weak", both mentally and physically.

Toormore went to Ireland for his final race of the season, raised up to Group 1 level in the National Stakes at the Curragh.

Hughes must have thought the colt had matured since Goodwood because he decided to set the pace from flagfall. To his credit Toormore kept focused on the job in hand, responding well when pressure was applied to beat Sudirman by two and three-quarter lengths.

Toormore – galloping in front of his many admirers

Toormore appeared to stay the seven furlongs well, raising hopes that the mile will not be a problem. The colt's pedigree, though, is a little less conclusive.

Toormore is out of an unraced daughter of Danetime from the family of Peace Girl, a winner of a 5f Group 3 as a two-year-old. His half-brother Try The Chance was best at trips up to seven furlongs.

Yet subsequent events showed the colt's form in a very favourable light. Goodwood runner-up Outstrip and National Stakes third Giovanni Boldini went on to fill the first two places in the Breeders' Cup Juvenile Turf at Santa Anita, while Sudirman later shaped well in the Middle Park Stakes.

Toormore is tough and progressive. He escapes a penalty for the Greenham Stakes so that is where he may start.

For all the claims of Toormore I would be more excited by his stable-companion **Night Of Thunder**.

You would not be expecting a son of Dubawi out of a mare by Galileo to show much pace at two, but that was far from the case when this colt made his debut in a 6f maiden auction stakes at Goodwood in October.

Travelling comfortably with the front rank throughout, he was nudged into the lead by Richard Hughes before striding away to beat a 74-rated rival, to whom he was conceding 7lb, by six lengths.

Just under a fortnight later he went to Doncaster for a 6f Listed race. Pitched in against Rufford, who was rated 107 having run second in a Group 2, Aidan O'Brien's very useful Stubbs and two other rivals rated 99 and 96, he took up the running a furlong from home before quickening clear to win eased down by three lengths.

Both races were run on soft ground and afterwards Richard Hughes was very complimentary, saying the 2,000 Guineas could be the target:

"That was very impressive. On that performance he could be a Guineas horse. Being on him it felt like top of the ground because of the way he travelled through the race, but the way he quickened was unbelievable. I am the wrong jockey to be asked about the ground after he gave me a feel like that. When a horse travels so well in a race and behaves so well as he did then they have to be good."

Night Of Thunder is the first foal of Listed-placed Forest Storm, a half-sister to 7f winner Tea Cup from the family of Irish 1,000 Guineas winner Forest Flower.

The Hannon team have a line to last year's top two-year-old form through Toormore, so it will be intriguing to see how the two colts are campaigned in early spring.

Night Of Thunder has shown speed and a turn of foot over a trip short of his pedigree requirements – usually a most encouraging sign.

The slight concern is that both his victories were on soft ground. He does, though, have a fairly low action and latest reports from the yard about his winter progress are very positive.

Shifting Power gives the Hannon team yet another possible Guineas candidate.

This imposing son of Compton Place made all to win an ordinary maiden auction stakes over seven furlongs at Sandown on his debut in July before following up in a 7f novice stakes – despite still running green - at Newmarket a fortnight later.

That form worked out well, with runner-up Treaty Of Paris winning a Group 3 race next time at York and the fourth winning a nursery off 85.

Shifting Power should stay at least a mile. His sire is an influence for speed, but his dam won over a mile and three furlongs and has produced three horses at stud that won over trips ranging from a mile and a quarter to two miles over jumps.

Shifting Power does not yet appear to have the class of Toormore

Night Of Thunder – could prove very smart

or the potential of Night Of Thunder, but he is very useful and entitled to take his chance in the Guineas.

Barley Mow, who impressed when winning his maiden at Newbury in August, then ran second to Be Ready at Doncaster before finding himself tactically outpointed in Group 1 company at Longchamp in October.

Anjaal is another top prospect for the yard. The son of Bahamian Bounty won the July Stakes on his third start before finishing three lengths adrift of War Command in the Dewhurst Stakes.

Paul Cole no longer attracts the quality of horse he once did but **Berkshire** should see him back feasting at the top table.

The colt shaped promisingly when a close third in a 6f maiden at Newbury in May – a race that turned out quite well – and then just over a month later he showed great improvement, despite racing keenly early on, to come from last to beat Bunker by two and a half lengths in the Chesham Stakes.

Afterwards the trainer said the colt would have been seen in an even better light if he got more cover.

Berkshire then had a three-month break and did not reappear until Newmarket in late September, when he started joint 11/8 favourite for the Group 2 Royal Lodge Stakes.

Once again he was held up last of the five runners, settling better this time. Two furlongs from home it looked as if he would come through and win but he then hung fire and it was only in the dying strides that he got up, beating fellow joint-favourite Somewhat by a neck.

Afterwards the trainer said:

"He looked a bit green having not run for a long time and probably forgot a lot of what he'd learnt. He was also unbalanced running into the dip but he stayed on strongly. He is very much next year's horse. I doubt he will have a trial before the Guineas."

Berkshire has already shown that he gets a mile well and he has the breeding to stay further. His half-brother Keenes Royale won over a mile and a half while his dam was a Group class performer at up to a mile and a quarter and comes from the family of Chester Vase winner Mickdaam.

Berkshire is a progressive colt with the scope to improve. He does, though, look more of a galloper than a colt with gears and a mile may not present sufficient a test for him at the highest level this season. Furthermore a line through Kingfisher, who finished last at Newmarket, leaves him about six lengths adrift of Australia.

Godolphin are sure to have a handful of colts to call upon.

Be Ready, a son of New Approach, could be one of their leading lights.

An encouraging debut second behind Somewhat at Newbury in August was followed by an improved effort when beating the well-regarded Barley Mow by three lengths in a 7f Listed race at Doncaster's St Leger meeting.

Be Ready kept on well there and the second then went on to give the form a bit of a lift when running better than his finishing position suggests in a Group 1 race at Longchamp.

Be Ready is closely related to a winner over a mile and a quarter and a half-bother to a winner over five furlongs. The dam is an unraced daughter of Gone West, so there is a mixture of speed and miling blood in his pedigree.

Be Ready is probably Group class but he has something to find on form and I would not be certain of his staying a mile.

Outstrip links in with a number of lines to last year's best two-year-old form.

Beaten a quarter of a length by Toormore at Goodwood, he then beat The Grey Gatsby in the Group 2 Champagne Stakes at Doncaster before running third to War Command in the Dewhurst Stakes. Then, on his final outing, he beat Giovanni Boldini by half a length in the Breeders' Cup Juvenile Turf at Santa Anita.

Outstrip is by Exceed And Excel and is the second foal of a Grade 1 winner over a mile and a quarter who is related to useful performers over that trip and more.

Outstrip is held on various lines of form but he is a reliable and versatile type who is proven over a mile.

Marco Botti has some interesting three-year-olds this season and **Lat Hawill** looks set to go places.

He ran just once last season, making his debut in a 7f maiden race at Newcastle in October. He could not have been more impressive, settled a few lengths off the pace on the far side of the pack before taking the lead on the bridle and quickly pulling clear to beat Poetic Choice by eight lengths.

The form was only ordinary – the second won a nursery two starts later off 63 – but Lat Hawill was most impressive and I expect him to be earning black type at some stage of the season.

Lat Hawill must have thrived in his early days, having cost just 10,000gns as a yearling before escalating to 230,000gns as a two-year-old. Although his dam is by the sprinter Primo Dominie, she won over a mile and a half and is a half-sister to top dual-purpose performer Overturn from the family of top-class middle-distance performer Connaught Bridge.

From the evidence of Newcastle Lat Hawill should stay a mile. It will be very interesting to see where the trainer starts him.

Those looking for a reasonable outsider could do worse than side with **Astaire**.

Kevin Ryan's colt has never run beyond six furlongs, but his half-brother won over a mile and his dam, an unraced daughter of Dansili, is a half-sister to seven winners including a winner over a mile and a half.

Astaire won five of his six starts last season, notably showing battling qualities to win the Gimcrack and then the Middle Park Stakes at Newmarket where a line through fifth-home Sudirman gives him a narrow edge over Toormore.

Astaire looked very tough last season but, despite encouragement from his pedigree that he will get a mile, he ran in the style of a sprinter. His trainer will probably let him have a crack at the Guineas with the option of dropping back to sprint distances if he shows he doesn't stay.

Free Eagle needs to rebuild his reputation following his six-length drubbing by Australia in September.

Following an impressive victory in a 1m maiden at Leopardstown in August, trainer Dermot Weld then spoke about him in glowing terms. The colt is a half-brother to the same trainer's Sapphire, out of a dam related to milers including Irish 1,000 Guineas winner Trusted Partner (not entered).

John Oxx's **Ebanoran**, a well-related son of Oasis Dream who won at the Curragh in October, and Ralph Beckett's Kempton winner **Lightning Spear** should have good seasons. Sir Michael Stoute's **Munaaser** is also likely to improve significantly on his sole start (not entered).

Clive Brittain has suggested that **Rizeena** may take on the colts rather than tackle the 1,000 Guineas. The last filly to win the 2,000 Guineas was Garden Path, way back in 1944, but the trainer has been rewarded for his ambition in a long and successful career and he may persuade the owners to take this less orthodox option.

Please refer to my thoughts in the 1,000 Guineas preview for my views. Put succinctly, if she does line up then she will figure.

From France Jonathan Pease may decide to let **Karakontie** take his chance at Newmarket. The son of Bernstein followed his maiden win with a short-head defeat by Bunker in a 7f Listed race at Deauville. A month later he won a Group 3 at Longchamp before returning there to win the Group 1 Prix Jean-Luc Lagardere, with Barley Mow back in fourth and fifth.

It would be significant if Andre Fabre sent **Age Of Innocence** over from France. The colt won a 6f maiden on his sole start last season but the race did not work out particularly well. An early trial will tell us more.

Fabre also has **Earnshaw** to call upon. He showed a bright turn of foot to win his first two starts – the second a Group 3 at Saint-Cloud – before returning there to find Ectot three-quarters of a length too good for him in the Group 1 Criterium International (not entered). **Galiway**, also trained by Fabre, is expected to stay at home for the French Classics (not entered).

CONCLUSION

Kingman and Australia look exciting prospects. Of the two I would favour Australia, as his is the more progressive profile. Furthermore he is bred to appreciate the stiff test which the Rowley Mile imposes on a colt in the spring. He is also versatile regarding the ground, while Kingman is bred for a quicker surface.

War Command may be best at trips short of a mile on quick summer ground but of the others Kingston Hill has to enter the reckoning. He would be the most suited to soft ground on Guineas day and, at 10/1 in February, he could be fair each-way value.

My pick from Richard Hannon Jnr's team is Night Of Thunder. It is most encouraging that Richard Hughes thinks he could be rather special and his price of 20/1 could look tremendous value if he has a good spring.

Berkshire appeals as the type who will be powering home at the finish. A good run from him will, as with Australia, see a significant contraction in his price for the Derby. Astaire and Free Eagle are others to consider.

To conclude, I want to stay with Australia for both the Guineas and the Derby. In his possible absence I would take on Kingman with Night Of Thunder and, in the hope of soft ground, Kingston Hill. Rizeena could complicate things if she were to switch here.

INDEX OF HORSES

Abseil 29
Adelaide 85
Age Of Innocence 29-30, 126
Agena 85
Al Thakira 109
Alyasan 30
Amazing Maria 94, 103
Anjaal 122
Anjin 67
Annus Mirabilis 85
Arab Spring 30-31
Astaire 124-125, 126
Astonishing 5-6
Astronereus 32
Asyad 32
Australia 81-82, 89-90, 112-115, 126
Ayrad 33, 89

Balansiya 6-7, 91, 95, 107, 110
Barley Mow 8, 122
Basem 33, 89
Be Ready 87, 123-124
Berkshire 87, 90, 122-123, 126
Betimes 109
Big Thunder 9-10
Bilimbi 68
Blue Hussar 10-11, 84-85, 90
Boy In The Bar 34
Bracelet 93, 109

Cambridge 94
Carla Bianca 11, 107-108
Carlo Bugatti 117
Cloudscape 12
Curious Mind 12-13

Danjeu 34-35, 88
Dark Days 35, 89
Dazzling 93, 108
Dorothy B 106-107, 110
Dutch Rifle 68-69

Earnshaw 126
Ebanoran 35-36, 88, 125
Ebasani 36
Economy 37
Ectot 89
Emirati Spirit 37, 89

End of Line 38
Endless Credit 69
Ensuring 39-40
Enzani 40, 89
Ertijaal 13
Evita Peron 40-41

Festival Theatre 69-70, 89
Folk Melody 109
Forever Now 41
Free Eagle 81, 83, 125, 126
Fun Mac 70

Galiway 89, 126
Gallante 41-42, 89
Gamesome 42
Geoffrey Chaucer 84
Giovanni Boldini 117
GM Hopkins 43
Great White Eagle 117

Hadaatha 44, 109
Hoist The Colours 71
Hors De Combat 44-45
Horseguardsparade 85
Hydrogen 88

Idea 45
Ihtimal 93-94, 108-109
Illinois 85
Impulsive Moment 71-72
Indian Maharaja 83, 117
Indonesienne 104
Indy 14-15
Integral 15-16

Johann Strauss 84
Jordan Princess 45-46
Joyeuse 95
Jupiter And Mars 88

Karakontie 125-126
Katilan 46, 89
Kingfisher 83
Kingman 85, 111-112, 126
Kingston Hill 82-83, 90, 117-119, 126
Kisanji 47
Kiyoshi 103-104, 110

Lacan 47
Lady Heidi 16-17, 109
Lady Tyne 18
Lat Hawill 48, 124
Laurelita 72
Lightning Spear 18-19, 125
Lucky Kristale 101-102

Madame Chiang 48-49
Mahsoob 50, 89
Man From Seville 73
Mange All 49
Mannaro 74
Marakoush 88
Marvellous 93, 108
Mekong River 85
Min Alemarat 50
Miss France 91, 95, 97-98, 109
Moscato 74-75
Munaaser 51, 125
Muwaary 19-20
My Titania 20-21, 93, 95, 102-103, 109
Mystic Blue 89

Naadirr 51-52
Night Fever 52
Night Of Thunder 85, 120-121, 126
Norab 52-53

Obliterator 21
Observational 53-54
Orchestra 85
Outstrip 124

Patentar 75
Pelerin 54
Postponed 22
Prince Gibraltar 89
Psychometry 76

Radiator 109
Rapprochement 54, 89
Red Passiflora 77
Renew 23
Rizeena 99-101, 109, 125
Royal Battalion 55, 89
Royalmania 105
Rye House 24

Sandiva 109
Sarpech 55
Scotland 25-26, 88-89

Sea Pride 56
Seagull Star 56, 88
Shankly 57-58
Shell House 93
Shifting Power 121-122
Sinkal 58, 89
Stampede 58-59
Stomachion 77-78
Sudden Wonder 87
Sweeping Up 59

Taghrooda 26, 92, 95, 107
Tahira 60
Tapestry 92-93, 95, 98-99
Tarfasha 92
Tested 91-92
The Third Man 78, 88
Toormore 119-120
True Story 27-28, 87-88, 90

Unforgiving Minute 61

Vallado 61
Vallarta 79
Venezia 62
Volume 28, 94-95
Vorda 105-105

War Command 84, 115-116, 126
Warrior Of Light 62, 88
Weld Arab 63
Western Hymn 80, 89
Wonderstruck 63
Wrangler 64

Zee Zeely 64-65